Jaime in Taos

Jaime in Taos

The Taos Papers of
JAIME de ANGULO

Compiled with a biographical
introduction by

GUI de ANGULO

City Lights Books
San Francisco

The photographs in this book are all from Jaime de Angulo's personal albums.

Grateful acknowledgment is given for permission to reprint material in the following collections:

Letters from the Chauncy Shafter Goodrich Papers: Courtesy, The Bancroft Library, University of California, Berkeley; Letters and a brief passage from *Lorenzo in Taos* by Mabel Dodge Luhan from the Mabel Dodge Luhan Collection, Collection of American Literature, The Beinecke Rare Book and Manuscript Library, Yale University; Letters from the Edward Sapir Collection, National Museum of Man, National Museums of Canada, Ottawa; and a letter to Ruth Benedict in *An Anthropologist at Work* by Margaret Mead, © 1959 by Margaret Mead. Reprinted by permission of Houghton Mifflin Company.

Frontispiece and back cover photograph by Roger Sturtevant.

Library of Congress Cataloging in Publication Data

Angulo, Jaime de.
     Jaime in Taos.

     Bibliography; p.
     1. Angulo, Jaime de—Correspondence.   2. Taos (N.M.)
—Intellectual life.   3. Authors, American—20th
century—Correspondence.   4. Anthropologists—United
States—Correspondence.   5. Linguists—United States
—Correspondence.   I. Angulo, Gui de.   II. Title.
PS3501.N569578Z48   1985   818'.5209   [B]   85-11025
ISBN 0-87286-167-8
ISBN 0-87286-165-1 (pbk.)

CITY LIGHTS BOOKS are edited by Lawrence Ferlinghetti & Nancy J. Peters and published at the City Lights Bookstore, 261 Columbus Avenue, San Francisco, California 94133.

I wish to express my gratitude to Sra. Mercedes de Andía who carefully preserved for me all the letters Jaime sent to his family

and Wendy Leeds-Hurwitz, whose researches have been so helpful to me

and most of all, to my sister Ximena, who found the Taos journals and The Witch *among family papers and let me use them.*

To Ximena

Table of Contents

Introduction

Jaime de Angulo y Mayo was born on January 29th, 1887, in a fashionable area of Paris near the Bois de Boulogne. His father and mother were wealthy Spanish expatriates, and he led a rather pampered childhood, cared for by a nurse who spoiled him and called him "monsieur." He was the youngest child, with an elder sister and brother.

The family was extremely devout, and when Jaime took communion around the age of twelve he expected a tangible event, something that he would feel. When nothing in fact happened it was a crushing disappointment to him, and he concluded that all his religious training had been lies. He came to detest Catholicism, and remained an atheist until his death.

Jaime had all along been something of a problem child, rebellious and undisciplined. When he was fourteen his mother died, and his father, a remote, silent, and extremely eccentric man, put Jaime in a Jesuit boarding school. Jaime regarded the school as a sort of prison, with its rigid discipline, physical hardship, and loneliness; and he never forgave his father, on whom he had doted, for putting him there. He regarded it as an act of tyrannical selfishness.

1

At the age of eighteen Jaime convinced his father (who seems to have been, rather than a selfish tyrant, a perplexed authoritarian, long suffering if unimaginative) to give him the money to go to the new world to make his fortune in the cattle business. He arrived in New York on April 1st, 1905.

Armed with an introduction given him by people he met on the boat, he took the train to Denver, Colorado, and within days he was working on a ranch as a cowhand. At first he was deliriously happy and proud, and wrote home detailed letters about the life, but soon he came to hate the taciturn cowboys, the hard work, lack of sleep, bad food and loneliness. He abruptly decided to go to Tierra del Fuego, for reasons that are hard to understand, and wrote his family to write him there.

Jaime arrived in San Francisco in August, and spent a week or so in a hotel in North Beach waiting for his boat. He was fascinated by the many racial groups he found there, Spanish, Basque, French, with all the accents that were represented, and particularly with the Chinese community. He wrote long letters home about it all.

He took ship, stopping in Guatemala and writing home about the Indians he saw there, and then, instead of going on to Tierra del Fuego, he went to Tegucigalpa, Honduras, with the idea of going into mining, or maybe the cattle business, or perhaps banana planting. There, stranded and without funds or letters from home (which were all on their way to Tierra del Fuego) he worked for the city of Tegucigalpa as a foreman to a work gang digging ditches for the aqueducts to the city generators. It was almost seven months before money came to enable him to return to a less depressing and backward country.

He returned by ship to San Francisco and within days of his arrival took place the famous San Francisco earthquake and fire—which he helped fight. By then, tired of wandering and hard work, he had decided to ask his father for funds to study for a profession. His father agreed, and Jaime chose medicine, entering Cooper Union Medical School in August, 1906. He did well and was extremely happy.

In the spring of 1908 Jaime transferred to Johns Hopkins Medical School in Baltimore. Within a short time he must have met his future wife, Cary Fink, a fellow student and one of the first "hen medics" in the country. Cary did a great deal to forward Jaime's intellectual development; she was a Vassar graduate, the daughter of a cultured Virginia family, and had advanced and enlightened ideas.

In the summer of 1910 Jaime returned to Europe to see his family; his reasons seem to have been twofold: to attend a Socialist convention at Hamburg, and to ask his father's blessing to his marriage with Cary. There may also have been question of his inheritance, which his father had kept, both to recompense himself for the expenses of Jaime's education, and because he felt Jaime was not responsible enough to handle it. These financial considerations were complicated by the fact that Jaime's brother, Manuel, had drowned in a shipwreck in the English Channel while Jaime was sailing over. There may have been question of an inheritance from him as well.

There followed a disagreement with his father on both the question of the inheritance and on that of his marriage: Cary was not a Catholic. The outcome is not clear; Jaime did marry on his return, and did acquire a sum of money. But he and his father did not communicate for thirteen years; his father said, supposedly, "You are no longer my son."

During his years at Johns Hopkins, Jaime became increasingly involved with nature, camping, the wilderness. He and friends built a chalet in the mountains one summer. He must have been glad, on graduation at the end of 1912, to have an offer of a job in genetic research at Stanford University in Palo Alto, at that time a country town—especially as he had always said he preferred research to practice.

One thing that Jaime did before leaving for the West was to get United States citizenship, awarded in Baltimore on October 2nd, 1912.

At Stanford Jaime and Cary soon met a number of intellectual and artistic people—one of whom, Henry Cowell, the composer, remained a lifelong friend. And he seems to have enjoyed his work. But letters sent to his sister at this time show a growing disillusion with science, and a growing unhappiness. At the end of 1913, for reasons no one really knows, the job at Stanford came to an end, and Jaime took his inheritance and entered into a partnership in a cattle ranch in Alturas, Modoc County, which lasted a year. Near Alturas, on the northeast edge of California, live the Achumawi, or Pit River Indians, and during this year Jaime got to know them, like them, and respect them. Later on they were to become one of the most important interests in his life, the subjects of his most intense study, and the people with whom he felt, in a certain sense, greatest affinity.

After selling his share in the cattle ranch Jaime returned to Carmel, where he and Cary had a house. In a short time he learned of land available for homesteading in the wild country below Carmel, beyond Big Sur, in the mountains. By 1916 he had taken out a homestead on a ranch there, which he called, for some reason, *Los Pesares*, the Sorrows. He was to live there off and on for the rest of his life.

In the summer of 1915, while Jaime was getting his homestead but living part of the time in Carmel, he met two young women from the East, Lucy Freeland and her sister Helen, who were running a rooming house near the beach. Lucy Freeland was eventually to be his second wife. At that time she was very unsophisticated and inexperienced, the typical product of an eastern women's college in those days. Jaime took a fancy to her, and took her on as a sort of protégée, teaching her about many of the things that interested him: botany, Chinese calligraphy (which he had learned from a Chinese friend in Baltimore), and perhaps mathematics and astronomy. He encouraged her to go back for postgraduate work at the University of California, and to take anthropology, a subject that had come to interest him. That fall she took his advice.

At that time Jaime was a very dashing figure, well known around Carmel—a rather fashionable and somewhat bohemian town. He was extremely handsome, and rode well, sometimes dressed like a Spanish vaquero. He had two Irish wolfhounds, and was altogether quite spectacular. He knew the poet Robinson Jeffers, and through friends he had made in Stanford he came to know everyone who could be said to be of interest in the area. Jaime always made contacts easily, and had a wide circle of friends.

But although he enjoyed cutting a figure in Carmel it was really the wilderness that was most important to him at this period, and during the next few years he lived in almost total isolation on the ranch, a day and a half ride (the last part on very rough trails) from Carmel. Visitors were few and far between, and the work very hard—although he did usually have someone living there to help. He must have taken time to study and read there, because he always had an active and inquiring mind, but how he managed it is hard to see.

A great part of the fascination in living this hard and isolated life lay, for him, in using his inventiveness to solve problems without store-bought equipment. He wrote in a letter that there seemed to be a primitive in him, needing this expression, which now had a chance to live.

In 1917 the United States entered the First World War, and very soon Jaime decided to enlist in the Army Medical Corps. After a short time at Camp Lewis, Washington State, he was sent to Mineola, New York, joining a project of the Air Corps to devise tests both to select pilots able to tolerate altitude and to weed out those psychologically unsuited to the stress of combat.

He was soon sent to Ann Arbor, Michigan, to study psychiatry for this project, but the army having lost his papers (so the story goes), he was unable to be reassigned, and stayed there—finally giving the course himself—until the end of the war.

Jaime returned to Carmel in December of 1918, and to Cary and his new baby daughter, Ximena, born that spring. He soon returned to the ranch to continue the homesteading, but before he left he had the opportunity to meet some people who would be very important to him in his later life: Alred Kroeber, head of the Department of Anthropology at the University of California in Berkeley; Paul Radin, also in the anthropology department; and Paul-Louis Faye, then an anthropology graduate student. They were all friends of Lucy Freeland, who was spending Christmas in Carmel, as many U.C. people did. Lucy Freeland, who was always called Nancy, had by then taken up anthropology and linguistics seriously, and was later to work several California Indian languages, both with Jaime and independently, under the name L. S. Freeland.

The next years were transitional for Jaime; he was finishing up the requirements for the homestead, and at the same time his marriage with Cary was slowly disintegrating, particularly under the stress of their disagreements about raising their child. And he was reading deeply in anthropology.

In the spring of 1920 Kroeber, with whom Jaime had discussed anthropology and psychiatry on a number of occasions (Kroeber was himself a lay analyst), invited Jaime to give a lecture at the university. At the same time Jaime had the opportunity to work with a Pomo Indian at the anthropology department, to study and analyze the Pomo language and devise a system of writing it. And that summer Kroeber hired Jaime to give two courses in the anthropology department, one The Mental Functions in Primitive Culture, and the other The Relation of Psychiatry to Anthropology.

The next two years were very hard. The failure of his marriage, the disapproval of the university community of his relationship with Nancy, which had by now developed into an affair, and financial problems weighed on him. In the fall of 1921 Cary divorced Jaime and left with Ximena for Zurich, where she soon was working with Carl Jung. That fall Jaime went to Alturas, California, on his first field trip, the trip he described in *Indians in Overalls*. That winter, an extremely severe one, he spent at the ranch, working over his notes, and also writing his first piece of fiction, *Don Bartolomeo*, about a family of California Spanish, their relationship to the Indians, and the fate that overtook them.

In the spring of 1922 Jaime sent out letters to all his friends in the world of anthropology searching for a job in linguistics. Kroeber had heard of just such a job with the Mexican government and recommended Jaime, who was given the assignment. Jaime arrived in Mexico City at the end of the summer, and by September was in Oaxaca; he worked a quite astonishingly large number of languages that winter, in spite of the fact that he had a bad case of malaria.

By spring Jaime was dying to see his daughter, and left for Europe, with the tacit agreement of Manuel Gamio, head of the project. However, through a complicated set of misunderstandings and ambiguous reports, Kroeber believed that Jaime had simply quit the job for which he, Kroeber, had recommended him, and he never forgave Jaime. In later years Kroeber went to quite considerable lengths to warn people of Jaime's irresponsible and unreliable personality.

On his way to Europe Jaime passed through New York, and while there saw Nancy Freeland, who was east on family business. They unexpectedly decided to marry, and Nancy went with Jaime to Paris, and then to Zurich, where they both worked briefly with Jung, and then on a trip to Spain and Morocco. At this point Nancy, who was now pregnant and not feeling well, left to return to Berkeley, and Jaime took a walking tour from near Burgos to Guéthary, France, where his father was living, to make his "submission" to him. He described this visit in the sketches called *Don Gregorio*.

From Guéthary Jaime returned to Zurich to work with Jung, in whom he had become extremely interested, and to spend time with his daughter.

Jaime's stay in Zurich was interrupted in about a month by a telegram from Nancy telling him of the Berkeley fire, the famous fire that destroyed much of the town and her own house, built in the hills and designed by Bernard Maybeck. Jaime immediately returned to oversee the rebuilding.

That was the fall that Jaime met Mabel Dodge Luhan, and her Taos Indian husband, Tony, who were spending the winter in Mill Valley. Tony was to be extremely important to Jaime for the next few years, and Jaime always remained fond of him.

Mabel was originally from Buffalo, had lived in Florence, and had had a salon in New York. She had gone to Taos, as many intellectuals and artists did at that time, and got involved with Indian affairs. She had met Tony Luhan, fallen in love, and married him. It was rather a *cause célèbre* both in bohemian circles and in the Taos Pueblo, where Tony suffered a degree of ostracism as a result. Nevertheless, the marriage continued happily the rest of their lives.

After the birth of their son, Alvar, Jaime installed Nancy in the new house. The house was barely finished, but Jaime felt tired and in need of a change, and Mabel, who was returning to Taos, suggested that Jaime come and visit, driving down with Tony, who was taking back their car. Mabel particularly wanted Jaime to meet D. H. Lawrence, who would be there. Mabel shared to a degree Jaime's new passion for Jungianism, and she may have thought that Lawrence would share it as well.

Jaime and Lawrence of course did not get on at all, as is

clear on reading the wonderfully funny passages in the book Mabel later wrote about Lawrence, *Lorenzo in Taos*. Her description of Jaime is probably the best that anyone ever did. The story she describes his writing at that time is certainly *The Witch*, a sort of sequel to *Don Bartolomeo*.

Of course while Jaime was in Taos he was thinking of the Taos Indian language, and hoping against hope that some way might be found to overcome the Indians' secretiveness enough to take it down. Working language was always a passion with him, a real obsession. He never had enough, and would work on two or three simultaneously. At the end of his life he was trying to arrange a way of taking down Hebrew, as though no one had ever studied it before.

As it came about Jaime did return that summer, with Nancy and the baby, and did take down the Taos language. That winter he not only worked over his notes on Taos, but continued working over the notes on the Mexican Indian languages that he had taken down in 1922—without pay, one of the problems of that job having been that he would receive no pay for work done on the project outside Mexico.

I think that Jaime's last trip to Taos was the one at the very end of 1924 to meet Jung, who wanted to visit primitive people in the United States. Jaime met Jung at the Grand Canyon, and it seems they drove to Taos, where Jung met Antonio Mirabal (Mountain Lake), the Indian Jaime had worked with.

During the next ten years Jaime lived in Berkeley, working a large number of California Indian languages, first with money provided by Jung, then with money of his own, and after that with funds from the Committee on Research in Native American Languages, headed by Franz Boas. Of the many people funded by the Committee Jaime received more than anyone, and did more languages than anyone—in spite of the unrelenting hostility of Kroeber.

During this period the house in Berkeley became somewhat famous, even infamous, in academic circles. It was a center of attraction for anthropologists and linguists both from the department in Berkeley and from elsewhere, people such as Paul Radin, Paul-Louis Faye, Robert Lowie, T. T. Waterman, Duncan Strong, Walter Dyk, Bronislaw Malinowsky, and others. In those depression years, with prohibition, the house was not only a center for anthropologists and linguists, though, but for an odd assortment of the kind of free-spirited generation that tended to exist everywhere, and the wild parties on the hill were well known. But the people who came to Jaime and Nancy's house generally had lively minds and interests in other things beside drinking and partying. I once heard it said that one never knew when going up to one of the Sunday afternoon open houses whether there would be a wild party or a quiet afternoon's discussion of linguistics. And a great deal of the time Jaime was hard at work downstairs, completely unavailable to visitors.

In 1928 Jaime wrote *The Lariat*, a story of Indians at the Carmel Mission in early days, and the fate of a priest who was determined to save their souls. A year or so later he began the series, *Indian Tales for a Little Boy and Girl*, for my brother and myself.

In 1930 the Twenty-fourth International Congress of Americanists was scheduled to be held in Hamburg. Jaime was naturally extremely anxious to go, but of course there was the problem of money. Jaime wrote Boas asking if there was any project on which he could be sent to earn the money, and Boas sent him to Mexico to work an Indian language there. Jaime worked up the Chichimeco language, took a plane to New York, and took ship for Hamburg.

At that conference Jaime met someone who was to be very important to him for the next several years, Hans-Jørgan Uldall, the Danish phonetician. Uldall was already scheduled to come

10

to California to work for the Committee, under Kroeber's direction. Jaime realized that if he did not move fast he would be left out of the situation, and he wrote Nancy to meet Uldall at the ship in San Francisco and invite him to stay at the house. Uldall and his wife Inge were guests from time to time during the next year or so, and went on field trips with Jaime and Nancy—as did many of their friends, anthropologists or not. Uldall also helped them with the phonetic aspects of their work.

During the last ten years or so the ranch in Big Sur had been simply a vacation spot where the family went, generally with friends, for short visits. But in 1933 Jaime decided that he wanted to spend more time there, and especially that he wanted a proper house there. Work was begun on the famous "stone house," actually of cast concrete, and on other improvements. That summer there was a frightful automobile accident, in which the car that Jaime was in went off the cliff in Torres Canyon, below the ranch, fell one hundred and eighty feet through the redwoods, and landed in the creek. Alvar, who was with Jaime, was killed, and Jaime spent all that night and most of the next day pinned in the wreckage, with a broken arm and leg.

In shock Jaime and Nancy did not return to Berkeley after he was released from the hospital, but went back to the ranch, withdrawing from the world. Although Jaime tried to continue with the research projects that he was involved in he found it impossible. He was troubled with constant pain, insomnia, and anguish, and soon began to drink heavily. At the end of 1936 the family returned to San Francisco for the winter, where Jaime and Nancy worked the Cantonese dialect of Chinese. We returned to the ranch the next summer to try to establish a dude ranch with friends. Personality problems and lack of dudes ended that, and there followed the famous episode of the "last cattle rustling in California," in which Jaime was arrested and tried for shooting the cattle of a neighbor who had allowed them to stray habitually on the ranch. Jaime was fined but not imprisoned.

In 1939 Nancy returned to Berkeley so that I could go to school, and after a short visit there Jaime left and returned to the ranch, where he lived until 1942.

During the war he returned to work in the shipyards—as Nancy did as well—but the marriage was deteriorating, and in 1943 Nancy divorced Jaime and he went to live in San Francisco, where he rented a tiny room on Telegraph Hill in the "Compound," a group of cottages and apartments known for its bohemian population. There he gave lessons to private students in languages, mathematics, astronomy, or any other subject that interested them. Probably at this time he began what he considered his major opus, *What is Language?* (never published). He also worked as a janitor for the Office of War Information, where a friend had got him a job.

Sometime around 1945 Jaime returned to the ranch, where he became the focus of visits by young people attracted to the Big Sur by the reputations of Henry Miller, Jean Varda, Emil White and others. Henry Miller wrote a description of him in *Devil in Paradise.*

In 1948 Jaime learned that he had cancer, and returned to San Francisco for treatment at the Veterans Hospital. From there he returned to Nancy's house, where she nursed him during his final illness. During 1949 Jaime gave the children's program on radio station KPFA based on *Indian Tales for a Little Boy and Girl.*. These stories were later published by Wynn.

When he was too ill to go to the station he continued work on various projects from bed, where he was also visited by a stream of young students and writers. When well enough he worked in the garden, making a little Japanese landscape. During this period he also did translations of Lorca's poetry, corresponded with Blaise Cendrars, for whom he had written *Indians in Overalls,* and Ezra Pound. Jaime's attitude toward Pound was that he was quite sane when he wanted to be, and altogether quite funny. At this time Jaime also wrote the sketches of his father, *Don Gregorio*. It is interesting that Jaime had tried to write stories about his father in the Thirties, and had abandoned the idea because he found his own style impossibly affected and coy. In ten years he had found the style that suited him.

He accepted with philosophy the horrors of treatment for cancer, and kept away from pain killers as long as he could in order to have his mind clear for working. He died in October of 1949.

In a letter written to Nancy from the hospital in 1948 Jaime wrote: "I have had my fill of both the sorrows and the joys of life and I am quite ready to join the dance of the atoms in interstellar space. . . . When I contemplate this dance of the atoms over such a fantastic range in time and space, all seemingly but an expression of pure mathematics, (which is what some people call godhead) I am filled with such a quiet emotion that all the sorrows and disappointments of my life dwindle almost to a vanishing point."

The Taos Papers

Part One

The First Trip

In September of 1923, while Jaime was still in Zurich working with Jung, and Nancy was in her house on Buena Vista Way, waiting for her first child, a fire started in the canyon behind the Berkeley hills. Fanned by the hot dry winds of fall it burned over the ridge and came down into the town, where it eventually burned some four hundred buildings. One of the first houses it took was Nancy's, built only three years before. She escaped with only the clothes she wore, losing her books, manuscripts, and all her possessions. Like many others she took the ferry to San Francisco and went to a hotel.

One of the first things she did, of course, was to wire Jaime that she was all right. He hadn't heard of the fire, but as soon as he realized what had happened he borrowed passage from Cary and returned to Berkeley.

He immediately set about having Nancy's house rebuilt, contacting Maybeck to have him look over Nancy's plans, and overseeing the carpenters, plumbers, tile-layers, and stucco men. He found it all extremely exhausting, as anyone who has ever built a house will understand, and after about three months of intense effort he was utterly drained.

Building the house was not the only thing that Jaime was doing from September to March. He was always a prolific letter writer, and he found time to send long, long letters to Cary, who remained a close friend for many years, and he made new friends who were to be very important for the next year or so—Mabel and Tony Luhan. In a letter sent to Cary a bit later, in June, he described how he had heard of them.

17

I met Tony and Mabel thru a woman, a friend of ours. Of course I had heard of them before. I do not know much of her life, yet—it is not her I am interested in, but Tony. I say I had heard of them, because her marriage to him, a plain Indian, not educated, a regular Indian in mocassins and long hair, made a good deal of noise and I once read an account of it by some sensational reporter in the Sunday paper.

The thing was badly written, in typical newspaperese, and it made a bad impression on me. I made up my mind that she was a notoriety seeker, and he probably some half-breed adventurer. But I was quite mistaken. Five minutes convinced me that it was a real thing, that she was deeply in love with him, that she had discovered for herself the real values of Indian idealism, and that she was sincere.

I think that she originally hails from the Middle West. Married young and went to Italy with her husband. She held a salon there, in Venice, I think. That husband died. She came back to America, and held another salon in New York. I think it was about that time that some litterateur wrote that thing, novel, or whatever it is: "Portrait of Mabel Dodge" (Dodge was her second husband). And I think it was based on a futuristic portrait of her which hangs in one of the exhibitions and made a stir. She has a strong personality all right. —Well, finally she went West, joined that colony of artists in the Southwest, married a man named Stein (I believe, or Stirner or some such name—a painter) and got interested in Indian welfare work. That's how she met Tony (Antonio Luhan). There she found a man she could not boss, she could not even budge one inch. She divorced Stirner and married Tony. . . .

Jaime had simply gone to visit Mabel and Tony where they were living in Mill Valley, and introduced himself. After that they corresponded, and Jaime went back and visited fairly regularly.

One of the first letters he sent Mabel is this one:

145 Shasta Road, Berkeley
December 29, 1923

My dear Mrs. Lujan,

The ballad is great! May I have a copy? I would like to send it to Zurich.

I had never heard of the *Laughing Horse* before. I thot that everything in that number was good (except May Austin's, *which I confess I was too prejudiced to read). Your story was splendid. That really gave the spirit of the Indian. Nancy said it brot her right back to Taos. She spent some time there a few years ago. She spoke of it as being exceedingly beautiful, strange, almost Persian or East Indian.

I would like to see more of Mr. Lujan, go walking with him, or sit in the sun with him. I had not seen him well, the first time, on account of the late hour. I find his face full of an illuminating beauty—reminds me of the middle ages—there were faces like that, then. There is something very strengthening and assuaging in his presence. I would like to see more of him, but I suppose I would bore him.

Happy New Year to both of you.

Jaime de A.

P.S. As soon as I get some time I am going to try to write some of my experiences with the Achumawi for you. It might go in the *Laughing Horse*.

*Mary Austin, author of *Land of Little Rain*.

Tony Luhan. *I find his face full of an illuminating beauty. . .*

Soon Jaime wrote Mabel that he was sending a story. Whether this was the same piece he had promised on his experiences with the Achumawi I don't know. In May of 1924 Jaime did publish an article "The Religious Feeling Among the Indians in California"—in *Laughing Horse*. He had sent copies of that manuscript both to Mabel and Cary— he had got in the habit at that point of sending them copies of letters that he thought would interest them both. But that isn't a story.

In the next enthusiastic letter he goes into his ideas on the differ- ence between the Taos and the Achumawi Indians.

around January, '24?

My dear Mrs. Lujan

I am taking the liberty of sending you a story. It is not primarily about Indians, but still it will give you some feeling of the atmosphere of the California tribes. While coming home last night and thinking about you and Mr. Lujan, I suddenly realized that you did not know anything about California and the Califor- nia Indians—and all the time I had been taking for granted that you did. They are so much less organized than the Pueblo peoples, so much less picturesque—all that is exotic and alluring in them is hidden away—even you with your understanding of the Indian's spirituality would be shocked and disillusioned, I think, at least that would be the first impression. Theirs is a very slow rhythm, I mean in a very low pitch, hardly differentiated from the very rhythms of nature, if you know what I mean by that.

I hardly dare look back over my last sentence. I think it has neither queue ni tête and is not English at all, but I think you will guess what I tried to say. Now Mr. Lujan, by his aura, gave me the feeling of something quite specialized, where the values of life have already taken a very definite form of expression, as strange to me as the Japanese, for instance, but crystallized and definite, quite far from the fluid state of psychological stuff of people like the Achumawi, the Miwok, the Pomo, the Wintun, the Maidu etc. etc. I wonder what would be Mr. Lujan's reaction to them? Perhaps he would be puzzled and would not understand them. You see, you must realize that something like four or five million years, let us say, separate his culture from theirs—I don't mean at all to be exact—I just say four or five millions years, as a sort of proportion to the slice of historical sequence that we are able to compute with certainty from early Egypt down to us—computing from that. Anyway you see what I mean. Gad! but I would like to see what his reaction would be . . .

Well, anyway, here goes my story. As I say the Indian material is only incidental, but it is the only thing I can put my hand on, just off, I mean the only thing I can trust—I will look around and find some other things in the literature and mark off passages for you.

Please try to read it before Thursday, so that I can take it back with me, because that leaves me without any copy at all. You can read it in an hour.

Yours sincerely,

Jaime de Angulo

Soon Jaime had got Mabel interested in Jungianism, his passion at the time. (He later turned more or less completely against psychoanalysis—at least he ridiculed it mercilessly for the rest of his life.) It's obvious that he had grown extremely attached to Tony, with one of those attachments to men, generally older or more experienced, who seemed to him to have knowledge or wisdom that he lacked. He was fond of Mabel, but as he wrote Cary, it was not her he was interested in, but Tony. He was also extremely concerned that Tony not be put off by an episode that had taken place in Mill Valley, in which Jaime had tried to give a sort of lightning bolt psychoanalysis to a young friend of Mabel's, with pretty upsetting results.

[To Mabel Luhan]

Just returned from the city where we both went to see Dr. Lynch—and found your letter in the mail box. That certainly "got over" better than the mss.—and though my impulse is to go to bed, I want to answer you a few words, if only to tell you that your letter is like a rending of a curtain, giving me suddenly a vision of certain things I didn't understand well.

I think all you say about my *magical thinking* is very true. Perhaps that is the interpretation of those dreams of mine. I *felt* no danger for myself in this plunging into the darkness of black and red think, but perhaps I was only being fooled by my own desire for the irrational and my intoxication with it. I still think there is no danger for me, but I am glad to be warned—at least to have it pointed to me what the danger might be, which I did not realize at all. Perhaps also that is the "too much excitement in the unconscious." Golly! but we have to be careful with this analytical powder magazine!

I must say you impress me with having a very deep knowledge of analytical psychology, by whatever road you have reached it. Intuitively, I guess—that seems to be your outstanding function.

Your letter has given me a great deal to think about. For instance, what you say about not mistaking spirituality and occultism (of course that is *my* danger,—and I didn't see it—thank you for showing me), and the *door to spirituality being thru the heart*. Quite true!

Now, for the first time, I see with my intellect (and remember, intellect being my major function, I can only be reached through it) I see with my intellect just where feeling "comes in," what its value is. I realize that this I just said, my last words, must bring tears to the eyes of anyone who is not a thinking type. The idea, they will say, of having to bolster up feeling with an intellectual value! as if it, in itself, as mere feeling, was not a value, a VALUE in itself. But not to a poor devil of a thinking type, like your humble servitor. Whereas, now, seeing how my thinking, my darling thinking may be endangered thru the lack of feeling, I am keen to get some feeling into myself, while before I was only academically interested in acquiring it, because I knew it was a minor function. Thus, you may perhaps, without knowing it, have just given me a tremendous boost in my analysis. Thank you, my analyst, thank you from my heart. See, I am already developing some feeling. The beginning of a "transference"— quite a superfluous one.

And thus is Don Antonio my saviour. Of course, I see it now, as I speak, it unfolds itself. Without knowing it I wanted black magic from him. He, not being a magician, quietly refused. He says: "I have only spirituality to give you. Take it or leave it—but don't give me headaches." Excellent lesson. Yes, yes, I see it.

Jung said all that to me, last summer, but I wasn't ripe to understand, then. I am more so, now. Not that I will give up my black and red thinking—it's too lovely—but I will be careful.

Well that was a great letter from you—and your dreams too. Only I am not going to analyze them. I am not going to analyze any one. I don't want to plunge any more people into the collective unconscious. I am getting properly scared. And the first thing I know I will really lose Don Antonio's friendship—and I really care for that—more than ever, now. You see, more feeling cropping up. Oh, me with feeling—I feel queer! You do write better letters than peace plans. More of them, please.

Lynch will operate Wednesday morning (Cesarian section) (only clean and sensible way to have a baby)—so if all goes well (and having seen him do it before I know all will go well) I will be able to take a run to my ranch while Nancy is comfortable in the hospital. —go down by the end of the week (next week). And I will absolutely refrain from any magic with Tony, I swear it, word of honor.

Well, off to bed to be back fighting with the plumber, the plasterer, the electrician, the carpenters and the rest of my enemies to-morrow morning bright and early.

You don't know how funny it is, really. Just imagine, the men who put on the lath are not the same as those who do the plastering,—not only that but the men who put on the lath inside are not the same as those who put it on outside—that's a totally different union. One man puts in the stove, another the flue and a third must make the hole for the flue, but none of the three know anything about the requirements of the man who is to put tile around the stove! And I, an amateur anthropologist and linguist, must try to coordinate them all together! That's where *feeling* comes in, I tell you. I want to curse them all and stamp on my hat, but that wouldn't do. Instead, I must smile— good night—

[unsigned]

Another letter that Jaime sent both Mabel and Cary had to do with Jaime's ideas on the difference between Taos and Achumawi attitudes toward magic.

Nancy wrote Mabel:

Dear Mrs. Lujan,

Jaime wanted me to jot down this reminder of our breakfast conversation of today—copies for you and for Cary. Here is yours. . . .

Nancy

This morning we were talking about Tony and how different he is from any of the California Indians we have met—how the whole outlook on life seems to be so different with the people of the pueblos from what it is here, especially with regard to magic—"power."

"Now for one thing," said Jaime, "take what Tony said about me—that I look like the devil in my red and black shirt. No California Indian would have said that. The idea would never occur to them.

They would never be afraid of me, either, or think of me as a sorcerer or a witch—someone who knows 'black magic.' There isn't any black magic and white magic with the Achumawi—any 'occult'—there is just power, and it belongs to anyone who can get it from the spirits.

Of course if a man is malicious and uses power to hurt people, they may be afraid of the man, but they aren't afraid of the power. I suppose that is why they are not secretive like the Taos Indians, and not afraid to talk about all these things, like who the sun is, and how to get power.

They are so primitive.

In the pueblos, everything is already very sophisticated. All the legitimate power—the white magic—is channelled into rites and ceremonies. It belongs to a priestly class. And anyone else who deals in power must be a sorcerer and deal in black magic. And all other people should be careful, should only touch the world of power thru these intermediaries. Shouldn't even talk too much about such things."

[unsigned]

On the copy that went to Cary, Jaime added this postscript:

I asked Nancy to write this out for me as I went out to work—I wanted it especially to show the difference, how much difference there is between the "pueblo" Indians (Southwest, so called) and the California tribes

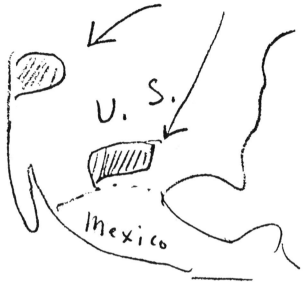

The "pueblo" very much advanced in culture, the California more primitive than even the Australian bushmen. Very few people realize that—this is therefore a good document. The Achumawi of Northern California for instance belong to a period that antedates the scission of magic into two branches of the white and the black.

Nancy had her baby, a boy, called Alvar, on February 6th. To Jaime's great joy he was able to install her in the barely finished house after her stay in the hospital. But his battles with the carpenters were not over until March, at which point he was completely exhausted.

Mabel was going back to Taos then, and she invited Jaime to drive down with Tony, who was taking back the car, and visit them. Jaime wrote Cary about it in the following letter:

Berkeley.
March 18. 1924

You must be wondering what has happened to me. Nothing except being buried under a house in construction. I had made my mind to have it completed, or at least far enuf towards completion, to tranship Nancy and her infant right into her rooms from out of the hospital. Well and I did it—let me crow! I have earned my crowing and cockle do-ing and ruckuckuing. When was it that we started the building? Somewhere about Christmas and it is now finished—just think—Nancy and Helen moved into their respective houses on the very same day, by a funny coincidence.

But the result is that I am worn out, ironed out, flattened out. I already had one breakdown just about a week before Nancy came home. Started out one day with that feeling of nausea at the very thought of work which I have learned to recognize as the danger signal to quit, and rest. But I simply couldn't afford to quit just then. I had to get her rooms and the kitchen finished—simply had to—break or no break. I did not want her to move into a rented house when she had been dreaming for so long of the fun of nursing her baby in *her own* house. So I dragged myself around for a couple of days, until I picked up a little more pep, and back to the fight with carpenters, plumbers, tile men, and patati and patata. I couldn't even find the material time to go over to the hospital—such a long trip, as you remember—so must content myself with telefoning—luckily she was doing very well—went along splendidly all the time—

I was camping, myself, among chips and shavings, pipes and monkey wrenches, did not wash my face for a week, with all my papers and clothes in gunny sacks strewed around—well picture to yourself the capharnaum.

Perhaps the most tiring part of it all for me, was having to exercise my newly born sensation function at such a rate of intensity. I had to *deal with form*, creatively, for the first time in my life, do it consciously I mean. I had to and I had to do it fast. This door or that window had to be changed to accomodate some mistake of the plumber, and I must create a new and harmonious form and do it *right now*, on the spot, I could not afford to have three carpenters at $8.50 a day, waiting until the inspiration came to me leisurely. Well, I could have done all that and easily, had it been a matter of dealing with concepts that have no form, no shape, no mass, whose existence is only made up of the "matter" of relations, of criss-cross hitchings, of bearings on this and that, and otherwise their matter, I mean their existence, is not. That I swim in and it never tires me. But this thing of "*form*," this new thing, was terribly exciting, and difficult to handle, running away at the slightest provocation, landing me in the midst of tangled masses where I was puzzled—and the strain of it! The sense of exhaustion every evening! and then to sleep, profound sleep, with a feeling that dreams did not matter, (and they were all unimportant as a matter of fact).

But it was all well repaid. When Nancy came home—she was so pleased with the house—and delighted with every detail.

Well, now I can go. Because I am worn out and I have accepted the invitation of the Lujans to go back with them to Taos (in New Mexico). Tony is going to drive the car all the way—I go with him. We start Saturday (two days hence).

Of course, there are a million things to be done here yet. I feel as if I were just hopping into a passing ship, just cutting off and leaving everything in desperation. I can't remain here and keep from working on the house—and I can't work anymore. So I am off.

Of course this is a grand opportunity from the point of view of anthropology and my field work. I don't expect to stay there long. Perhaps a month. And I don't intend to work—just loaf. But as Nancy says, in Indian field work the second time you come you are an "old friend," and everything is smoothed out, and confidence established, no matter how little you stayed the first time. Thus, a man who goes and stays only a week, then goes back a year after, that second time the Indians feel more confidence for him than they would at the end of six months the first time.

I may never find anything of interest to my special line of research, among the Pueblo Indians. I feel that they are too civilized, almost as much as the Aztecs, or the early Greeks. My Indians are the California tribes, real primitives with the "wonder stuff" loose and free on tap. Still you can't tell. Deep in my heart there is an ambition that I may be able to reach that group of old men, the Keepers of the Faith, I think that's the name that Bandelier gave them, unless I am mixing it up with something else. A group of old men who spend all their time fasting. They take no heed of worldly matters, are not consulted about the direction of the affairs of the tribe, never appear in council, but they are the ones who keep in touch with the "Powers Above" and the whole tribe through them. And they, of course, come out of their contemplation in time of religious ceremonies. Now I feel it in my bones that they know a great deal about the translation of certain powerful elemental forces into safe symbols—things that are not revealed to the common run of the tribe, even to the initiated men. Frankly, I don't think I will ever get there. How could I hope to obtain what is revealed only to mature Indians after years of observation of their conduct and trial?! Unless I were the Quezahualcoyotl himself with his white face and blond hair. All joke aside, I don't think it possible (although I think that the Zuñis did reveal something like that to Cushing. But he lived all his life with them. Besides the Taos people are even more distrustful than the Zuñis, Kroeber says.)

Well, anyway, I am off. I think Nancy can get along. She is in fine health—so is Alvar, and the house is still full of carpenters and they are all very fond of her and anxious to do things for her. Besides there is one German, working for us, who is going to stay on the job till I come back, and I can trust him thoroly. . . .

Well, adios—my address will be care of Mabel Lujan, Taos, New Mexico.

Tell Jung that this is not to be regarded as a field-trip. I will not use any of the field money on it—unless it should develop something worth while, something that would justify it.

In 1932 Mabel published a book, *Lorenzo in Taos*, about D. H. Lawrence's visit to Taos, and their friendship. She also put in a description of her stay in Mill Valley, of Jaime's visits there, and his stay in Taos. For some reason, instead of saying that Jaime drove down with Tony she implied that he just turned up!

[From *Lorenzo in Taos*]

Quite suddenly Jaime arrived in Taos. He strode in one day on his rope-soled sandals, his small Spanish feet twinkling in wide, Mexican trousers, his blue béret far back on a head of long, crinkly hair.

Jaime was prepared to worship Lawrence as a hero, and he was determined to impress him. But perhaps Lawrence was prejudiced against him in advance. Although at first Jaime flattered him by attending to him every instant, after a very few days

Lawrence was scolding and snubbing him. Of course Jaime, like most other people, had misinterpreted Lawrence's writing and he attempted to please him in the very way Lawrence couldn't endure!

Lawrence himself was outspoken enough, to be sure, but he didn't like other people to be so; particularly he disliked uncouth language from other men. So when Jaime called women bitches, Lorenzo just squirmed. And when Jaime tore off his shirt in the dining-room one day after lunch and strutted up and down, showing what fine muscles he had in his back, Lorenzo looked quite pale and sick and ran out of the room.

"He's not quite all right," he told me, presently. "You must keep an eye on him. Next time he'll rip his trousers off, I wouldn't wonder!"

We all went soon to the hot springs together. When the men came out, Tony was laughing and Lawrence was in one of his rages again, while Jaime was oblivious to both of them. He was declaiming about the magical atmosphere down there, and he said:

"As soon as I entered, I recognized the Power . . . the collective unconscious."

"What's the matter?" I whispered to Lorenzo at the first opportunity.

"He started saying his *prayers* or something, in the water!" replied the incensed Lorenzo. "Closed his eyes and stretched himself out and began to murmur! 'It's the sacred Indian word,' he explained, opening one eye and then relapsing into it again. It's insulting! A man has no business to be so indecent in a nice hot spring like that."

Lorenzo was simple. He demanded that other people be as simple as himself and never expose themselves as Jaime was always doing, both inside and out! Probably he felt the wonder of the place even more than Jaime did, but it was unthinkable to him that anyone should forget himself and let his ordinary everyday behavior be replaced by an outré impulse to pray! I think you can understand how he felt about that, Jeffers. He was always not only outraged, but pained if anyone acted *queer*! And he felt so sorry for anyone who hadn't enough sense of humor to prevent himself from being ridiculous that he hated him!

Jaime began to resent Lawrence's treatment after a while, so then he turned his attention to Frieda; and she, nothing loath, responded with crescent-shaped smiles and began to primp herself. Lawrence couldn't bear it!

One night after supper when Spud and Tony and Jaime were all there and Ida was up from Santa Fe on a visit, Lawrence jumped up from his chair and ran up to Frieda, who was joking with Jaime, a cigarette dangling from the corner of her mouth. And he began to shout invectives at her, calling her a bitch and so on. And he so out-Jaimed Jaime that the latter was speechless for the rest of the evening. The next day he told me Lawrence was a red fox, and that, after all, Frieda was much the more important of the two, much more of a person.

"None of you people around here appreciate her. You're all *hypnotized* by Lawrence. He's nothing but a neurotic!"

However, he couldn't bear to give up. He ceased to try to impress the man and began to compete with the writer. He produced pounds and pounds of paper and arranged a writing-table in the wide window of the log cabin, where, from the el that juts out from the main, long house, he was in plain view of everyone coming or going. There he sat, bent over a typewriter all day long for days and days. When we went out, we saw him, and when we came in, we saw him. He would lift a pale face and glare balefully out at us without a sign of recognition.

It kept Lorenzo giggling. He called Jaime "your captive author," and, indeed, he looked like a poor imprisoned devil who had so many pages to do before he could be freed. At meals he scarcely spoke, but stared at his plate in silence.

"He is acting like a writer, I suppose," tittered Lorenzo once.
Finally Jaime came in one night with a roll of manuscript.

"I should like to read it to you," he said, in a low, even voice, with an air of "I don't need to say anything; I can let it speak for itself" about him. We were polite. We grouped ourselves around the fire in comfortable chairs, and Jaime started to read.

I suppose it was autobiographical. And it was meant to be awesome. There were dark pools at the bottom of the garden; there was a monster, half man and half toad; and it went on for pages and pages. My mind wandered and I watched the others. Lorenzo was playing with Lorraine's ears; Frieda was smoking and knitting; Tony was asleep; and Ida was staring at Jaime with a puzzled glint in her large, horn-rimmed spectacles. What was it all about? Would it never end?

"My mother! Oh, my mother!" wailed the monster in Jaime's Spanish voice; and Lawrence flecked me a little look as much as to say: "The *preposterous* fellow!"

The fire was out and the room was cold when he stopped reading. To this day I don't know what he read. I never listened less to anyone, and that is saying much! Jaime was confident he had hit a bull's-eye.

"Well," he said, getting up and trying not to look proud of himself.

"Yes, my dear Jaime, but is it not rather long?" queried Lorenzo.

The last of him was seen the day we all went to the dance at Domingo. He had bought an Indian serape, broad dark-blue and white stripes. He said he was going to walk home from there to Berkeley. Just like that—he with his new serape over his shoulder!

I am sure he never believed we would let him—but we did. Towards sunset he started west when we turned eastwards to Santa Fe: a tiny figure on the broad highway, with his blue béret and his rope-soled sandals, looking so solitary and yet with a kind of courage and panache about him.

"How could you, Mabel! He never meant to do it!" cried the tender-hearted Lorenzo.

What Mabel and Lawrence probably didn't know was that when Jaime had been living in the wild coast country of Big Sur he had often walked some fifteen miles round trip to get his mail, or walked seven miles to the ranch from Pfeiffer's to get the horses and then ridden them back to where the car was left. He had always been a great walker; the year before he had taken that walking tour through Spain from around Burgos to see his father and sister in Guéthary. Anyway, he never meant to walk all the way to Berkeley! He meant to hitchhike.

When Mabel's book, *Lorenzo in Taos*, came out, in 1932, of course Jaime rushed to get a copy. He read part of her description of him, and then called up a family friend, Roger Sturtevant, in an absolute rage. He'd get her, he said, he'd write a rebuttal that would show the world what kind of a person she was, etc. etc. A few days later he called back, having finished the book, and said, "You know, I don't have to write anything. She said it all herself."

A few years later, when Mabel brought out her memoires, she sent the manuscript of the first volume to Nancy and Jaime at the ranch, where we were living then. Jaime found it fascinating, and it served to help him pass what was the worst time of his life. In one of her letters she evidently expressed some sort of bad conscience about her portrayal of Jaime in *Lorenzo in Taos*. Jaime wrote her:

Nov. 2, 1933

. . . And how we were sorry when we closed the book, and wished the second volume were out. Oh! Mabel, you are always interesting, whether in real life or the printed page. Just like your *Lorenzo in Taos*. We read it last year and roared and roared over it. And by the way, why should you have a bad conscience about me? I thoroughly enjoyed the caricatures you made of Frieda, and Bret, and Clarence, and worst of all, of yourself. So why should I not enjoy my own caricature? Every line of it was true—oh, except one, a mere detail, but it got my goat, so let's have it out and have it over with. You gave the impression that we had invited ourselves: had you forgotten how you invited us and invited us and invited us? Well, it's a small matter—when you read a book it is all easy—when you write it, it's different. But can you imagine either of us who pride ourselves on our breeding above all else, doing that?

Well, as it so happens, Mabel was not the only person to write an account of that visit to Taos, although I don't think she ever knew it. Jaime wrote Nancy a long running letter about his visit, and he sent Cary a carbon copy of it. Nancy never kept letters in those days, and her copy disappeared. But Cary kept hers. Jaime wrote:

Taos—date? 1924
first week of April—I think

I am here at last, as the portals of the mysterious Taos, Taos out of which the anthropologists have never been able to get any information, and I never shall, either, I don't think! I have not been in the pueblo yet. Mabel's house is in the village, five miles from the pueblo. I will not go to the pueblo until Tony takes me there himself. Good old Tony—our friendship is now cemented for good—and between our two wills there goes the silent battle. I will not ask him but I want to know. He knows I will not ask him any questions, and he turns around and around almost plaintively. He is forever at it. He brings it up himself. We sat in a cafe, eating our supper in Albuquerque. There was an Indian design painted around the room. "The whites don't know what that means," says Tony suddenly. "No, they don't," say I. Silence. Then "Do you know? "No, I do not." "But you would like to know." "Yes, I would." "But haven't I told you that my box is locked? I will never tell you anything." "I have not asked you to tell me a single thing yet, have I?" "They'll say I tell everything to the whites, because I married a white woman."

Another time in Zuñi, he took me to the house of a man named Zuñi Dick, a good worker in shells. Tony did some bartering with him, shells he had brought from California in exchange for turquoise rings, etc. Zuñi Dick spoke English fluently, talked much, seemed to know a good many white people, anthropologists, traders, welfare workers, etc. I sat mum. When we left, Tony said "How do you like him?" "I don't." "He will tell you things." "He will tell me lies, too." "Maybe. They talk here in Zuñi. That's the way they are. Maybe they tell you if you ask." "I don't ask." "Well, there will be no use your asking in Taos, because you won't find out anything."

In Zuñi again, in another house, he started to talk politics. He had said they could speak before me. "He is not like a white man. He knows all our things." They went on rehashing the old quarrels between the two factions in the pueblo. They complained that one of the delegates to Washington had "sold ceremonies" to Hodge at the Bureau of American Ethnology. Now the pueblo has forced him to leave, etc. etc. "What are you kicking for, now!" said Tony. "It's too late. Why did you allow them to take photographs? You let the whites come to your ceremonies. Now everything is known. It's too late now. What are you kicking about. It is your own fault. You let Cushing stay here. You let him build a house. Then you told him everything, what this altar is for, what this drawing means, this thing, that thing. Then he published it. It is all in books. I have seen them. It's all open now. In Taos we don't tell anything. We don't show anything. It's all secret. It's all under."

37

Another time he said to me, "You like Coyote very much, don't you?" "Yes, it's my animal." "Coyote is very clever, he is very malicious. Coyote wants to know everything. Always to know, to know. What good does it do to know. What for do you want to know. Those things belong to the Indians. They are not for the whites. What can the whites do with them? The Indians have got to have them because they do something with them, but the whites want to know just for curiosity." "No, Tony. I don't want to know just for curiosity. I want to know because I think the whites have lost their soul and they must find it again. Some of the things the whites have lost, the Indians have kept." "Yes," Tony interrupted, "we know the explanation of how everything is. We know what the sun is, and the moon, and where men came from, and why this plank here is. We have kept all that. We know many things the whites don't know. But I will never tell you." "I have not asked you." "You can ask them in Taos, maybe they will tell you." "No, I won't ask anyone. They can tell me if they want to. You know I want to know and you know I will not publish anything. You know I will not tell anyone except that man in Switzerland and he will never tell, but he can do good with it, he can do things with it. I am going to Taos as your friend. I will not look at anything. I will not ask any questions. I will not even learn any language, altho you know that's my greatest pleasure. I don't want you to tell me anything. If you think it is good I should learn, tell the old men and if they are willing they can tell me."

Jung

The whole atmosphere here is strange, imposing, too vast in its rarefied cold air. We must be about eight thousand feet above sea level. And the mountain towers still higher above this immense plain, the top covered with snow. So, you feel, after climbing and climbing from plateau to plateau, in this land of high cold deserts, after passing through all these pueblos, each more and more remote from civilization, after going up the Rio

Grande, the same Rio Grande that we had already seen, a majestic river, way back in California, here a small river, after leaving the last of the Tewa pueblos, and climbing up through the cañon, rough with boulders and the rushing stream, at last you emerge on this immense plain, still higher than everything, and Taos nestling at the foot of the mountain, you feel that you have come at last to the remotest of all the pueblos, to the last citadel, impregnable behind its wall of morose contempt for the futility of the white man's knowledge.

Even if I should ever get anything, even if I had permission to publish I would not do it, I believe. I would not for this reason: because I begin to see clearly that the life of the pueblo community is inextricably tied to its ceremonies. The Pueblo Indian is millions of years removed from the California Indian. Ever so many forms of libido that still function freely in the interactions between the California Indian and the mother nature, the free accessible spirit-stuff as I call it, has become locked in symbolism, ceremonial symbolism, and community ceremonial at that, in the case of the Pueblo. Now, the moment that esoteric symbol is opened, revealed, published, it will become a dead sign, exoteric, a museum thing—and the Indian will die—die because [he is] not at the proper place in the procession of cosmic events, as we were when *our* symbols became dead, with the rise of rationalism, but we were ready for the change and the loss, and the interregnum of dead materialism, preparatory for a new dispensation, a new recombining of psychological elements—if I get any stuff that will help Jung I will give it to *him*, but I will not sacrifice the pueblo of Taos for the sake of museum anthropology.

But let me go back to the pueblo of Zuñi where we were snowbound for four days, and give you my impressions. I did not like Zuñi at all. In the first place the language is hideously ugly. That is certainly not a tone language! It sounds like the mouth full of sticky mush, with the syllables exploding thru it, in a sort of staccato, hacked off between glottal catches.

The women are so ungainly! They don't walk, they wabble in a painful, ponderous manner, and what with the bulky blanket dress coming only to the knees, the immense silk handkerchief hanging gracelessly from the shoulders and the fact they have nearly all discarded moccasins for high-heeled laced boots with fat calves popping out of them, they look like erect beetles. Even the few who still wear moccasins have the same ponderous, draggy, ungainly gait. Even very little girls drag themselves about in that heavy manner. I would be tempted to formulate a theory that the Indian women make their sexual appeal thru the idea of the mother, mother Earth, large, heavy, slow, immovable, permanent, a safe abode. But immediately I remember the Zapotec women so nimble and graceful. The Pueblo men on the contrary are very light and graceful. It was cold and they all went about wrapped in their blankets. That is another of the characteristic marks of pueblos, just as in the Zapotec pueblos, those figures gliding about, wrapped to the eyes. It contributes to that general atmosphere of secretiveness and furtiveness that permeates pueblo life.

But Zuñi generally gives me a sensation of disintegration. There is no question but that the old life is disappearing. I noted that very few people there speak Spanish. Quite a few of the men speak English, at least brokenly, but the greater number even of rather young men do not speak anything but Zuñi. Of the women only girls of ten to fifteen know any English.

While in Zuñi we spent a great deal of the time singing. It would appear that Tony is somewhat of a specialist. He had a lot of "new songs," songs composed last year in Taos, songs also that he himself had composed during the winter. There was a bunch of Zuñi young men who were keen to learn them. Tony would take the drum and commence singing, song after song, hour after hour, sometimes past midnight. Some were frightfully difficult and no one could get them. I found that I was better at it than some of the Zuñi men, but slower than the most. As far as I could see the songs they found difficult were also the ones I found difficult. We sat in a circle around Tony. The first few times Tony's voice went on alone. Then gradually there was an increase of volume and finally everyone became bolder and we all sang and beat time lustily and we felt fine. While we were driving through the desert, Tony at the wheel, he would sing for hours and hours, song after song. He sang many medicine songs for me. But to the Zuñi boys he only sang dancing songs. I have become so accustomed to that music now, that I have come to wonder whether the scale is really different from ours. Of course it must be. What am I talking about! Yet it seems impossible that in so short a time it should have lost all strangeness to me. I mean that all those notes seem quite all right and natural to me. It is hard to believe that they are the same ones that used to produce such a strange impression on my ear that I thought they would always sound queer. The Pueblo Indians, singing is certainly a very important part of their life. And it is only the men. I don't know whether the women sing at all. I don't think they do. At least it is not a serious occupation, a definite thing, as it is with the men who gather and do nothing but sing for three or four hours consecutively.

In Zuñi, I cemented a strong friendship with the cacique Justito, an old man who is also a wizard. He and Tony bargained for a long time over a "caballito," one of those charms, you know, a small stone crudely resembling an animal, which he extracted from a pouch containing sacred corn meal. He said he had worked all winter on it and it was very powerful. Finally he let it go, but warned Tony not to let any Zuñi man see it. All this went on half in broken Spanish, half in sign language.

His daughter, a middle-aged woman (she belongs to the Bear totem, Tony told me) admired very much my blanket. The next day I went alone to their house to bring them an abalone

41

Probably Cacique Justicio. . . . .an old man who is also a wizard.

shell for a present. Once more the woman admired my blanket and I felt impelled to give it to her. The old man then told a younger girl to offer me a silver ring with a turquoise, but I would not take it. I also refused a silver bracelet with three turquoises on it. Then he offered me a caballito. I told him it was no good to me without the words. I got a curious glance at that. He was silent for a while. Then he began again to say that he wanted shells and feathers. "I need shells and also feathers for ceremonies. You go California. You come back, bring feathers, feathers pheasant, feather parrot, hard to get in Zuñi. You go back California. Remember cacique Justito. You think cacique Justito. I think you." Then he went to the wall and took down a very good photograph of himself, and he pressed it against his belly and then gave it to me. "You take it. Go back California. Make you think cacique Justito, your friend, he think hard for you, you look picture, you think Justito, bring back feathers, feathers pheasant, feathers parrot, long tail feathers."

It was just then that Tony came in. He pretended to be very hurt. "What is the matter with me? Why don't you give me your picture? I am not a good friend." Later on Tony said to me, "That old man has got lots of power. I am afraid of them in that house. What did you do to him to make him give you his picture. He must like you very much. Now you have got his power. That woman has got lots of power. She always gets what she wants. Last year when I came thru Zuñi she got a blanket out of me just the same way. When she wants to talk to the spirits she goes up in the air."

After Zuñi we went to Isleta, where Tony has some relatives. The language of Isleta is, I think, the most musical and harmonious I ever heard. I am pretty sure it has pitch tones.

In Isleta I saw a woman (the wife of a cousin of Tony) who was exceedingly graceful in all of her movements. In her moccasins (with the buckskin wrapped leggins) and blanket coat and red belt, she reminded me of the pictures of Esquimo women.

All her movements were full of grace and lightness. I could not take my eyes off her. But she is a solitary exception, so far.

We spent a night in Santo Domingo. The Indians there somehow looked very barbaric. They use more red paint there than in any of the other pueblos that I have seen en route. Some of the faces were almost vermilion. (Tony made me paint my face in Zuñi. "Now the women will like you.") In every house there is a flat slab of stone, and a small chunk of red stone which you grind on the slab. Then you rub it on your face, especially two thick dabs in front of the ears, and a dab under the lower lip. At any time you may see a man go to the stone and redden his face just as unconsciously as our women powder their noses.

The language of Santo Domingo is chuck full of epiglottalized consonants. Not tonal, at least not markedly so.

But at San Juan (Tewa, on the Rio Grande), I heard a language so full of tones, and with so many nasals that I could imagine it was Chinanteco!

Well, Mabel has here an enormous establishment, five or six houses, helter skelter as you may imagine, full of valuable Indian things in great disorder. One of the houses is occupied by D. H. Lawrence and his wife. I like him very much, strange duck that he is.

I have been here three days and four nights but I have not seen the pueblo yet. Yesterday we went riding, Lawrence, a queer English girl who lives with them, and I. They went to the pueblo, but I turned back. Lawrence sneered at me for that. He thinks I am posing.

This morning at breakfast Mabel announced we would go to the pueblo. "Oh, but I forgot, today most of the men have gone to the mountain. But that does not matter. You will see the pueblo anyway, and we will go and see Tony's mother." I said nothing. I told a dream I had during the night. The light of the fire suddenly flared up and nearly woke me up. Someone said to me, of the fire, "That's one of the ceremonies you are

Las Palomas in 1985. *Mabel has here an enormous establishment . . .*

looking for." I said, "That's no good. It must come to me through Tony," and I turned around and buried my head in the blankets not to see the fire. Then I dreamed I was in a tropical forest. I was traveling with another man. We were sent on an important and dangerous mission. There was a Malay with us, a very dark, wiry, little man. He was our body-guard. We were lying on the ground, resting, in that dark tropical forest. There was danger lurking about. I was lying with my eyes shut. I said to my companion, "Those men have to be destroyed. They have rebelled against their king." There was no answer. I sat up. My companion was gone. I said to the Malay, "He behaves badly. He should not go that way, without telling me." I became aware of increasing danger. I must be keen and alert. I must become a black man. I must enter into the body of that Malay. I said to him, "Balang, you must make my belly strong so that I may crawl on my belly for miles through this forest." He started to tremble with emotion. He spoke to me like soothing a child and at the same time as if afraid of me. He began rubbing my belly with his hand. A great peace came over me, and a sense of strength. At the same time I became more conscious of dangers in ambush. He made me lie down and wrapped me in blankets and told me to rest and he would watch. He was crying. I knew he had been sent to kill me, but now he could not do it because I had made him give me his strength.

After breakfast, Tony took me outside the house. We stood against the wall in the sun. The mountain seemed immense. Tony said, "Do you feel that something important is going on? They are doing a ceremony for the benefit of the world. Nobody knows. It is very secret." "Why are you not there?" "Because I do not belong to that clan."

I said, "Look at the mountain now. The top is hidden in the clouds." He said, "Don't those clouds come from the sea?" "Yes, but the sea is very far from here. I feel strange here. I don't understand the spirits of this place. I can't talk to them. They are too far." "Look at the mountain," said Tony, "the spirits are not far there. You see that peak there, on the right, there is a lake there. You will go there, sometime." "Maybe I will. I don't know. I have come here not of my own will but something pulls me. Maybe the spirits will talk to me. I want to find out something which I must know. Maybe I am not ready for it, yet. I don't feel well, here. I am too far from the sea." "The sea is asleep," said Tony. "It will not wake up until the end of this world. You are afraid. That's the way I was in California. The spirits of this place rule the world. They are on top of it. They are powerful. They have talked to you in your dream. Do you want to come to the pueblo today, with us?" "Tony, I am not a tourist. I have not come here to look at curios. You know why I came here perhaps better than I know myself. I do what you tell me." "Stay here. You and I go alone, sometime."

They are gone. This plateau is immense. Spring is just stirring. The air is so dry it is almost brittle. Here there seems to be nothing but earth and vast mountains and sky with clouds. Nothing else counts. Too small. And a bunch of people who seem to have survived merely to perform a necessary ceremony.

I heard Tony say a few words to an Indian, this morning. There is certainly pitch tones. I caught several unrounded back vowels, and surd l's. But no epiglottalized consonants. By the way, in the language I heard at San Juan, I noticed that some consonants were pronounced with great *stress* but without being epiglottalized. At least I could not hear any crack.

Taos, April 9, 1924

Dreamed by Tony.

I dream last night. I am hunting birds, all kinds of birds. There are two other men with me, I think one of them is you, Jaime. Then a game warden come, he stop us, says is not allowed shoot there. Is a big mountain, lots trees and woods, I think it's back in California. Is another house, a square house in the middle of desert, nothing around, all dry like here. I can't stay in that house. A river, to the east of river is that house in the desert. We were hunting in mountain country, the other side of river. Hunting birds, all kinds. You remember in Zuñi you say you dream something about old man and woman who are keepers of the Birds (I am sorry I have forgotten now what it was) and I tell you is keeper of the Birds that old man, old cacique Justito. I think is same birds.

Taos—April 9

Tony took me to the pueblo yesterday, on a formal visit of presentation to the Governor. But the Governor was absent. Then he took me to the highest house top of the village. We climbed the ladders, from one house top to another, until we stood way above with the whole village under us. There was one man already standing there, silent. I recognized him as Joe Bernal, a man with a curious face marked by suffering. He came to see Tony, the other day. I noticed immediately a very panther-like appearance of his whole gaunt body, and something dark and burning in his personality. Mabel whispered to me, "Watch him, you will be interested in him. He knows a great deal about magic. Tony is afraid of him." Well, he nodded to us on that house top, but never said a word. We stayed there a long time, in silence. Then we went down and Tony took me to see his mother and his sister and nephews. After that we returned home.

This morning this Joe Bernal came into my room with Mabel. He had asked her to bring him. She left us alone. We smoked for a long time in silence. Then he spoke in a veiled and dark manner about the Sun our father and the Earth our mother, and also the Sea is our mother, very deep and very far, and men have forgotten many things but I live in the ancient manner, etc., etc., and he watches me when I come and he likes me because I am quiet and he is very poor but he thinks in his heart etc., etc. and he has never seen the sea but maybe I have been there, maybe I come from there. I took an abalone shell out of my sack and told him that came right from the sea. I gave it to him. He took it with great emotion and put it to his ear as if trying to catch some message, then he secreted it under his blanket and thanked me. And he went.

Later Mabel said, "He is a very strange individual. The Indians do not like him. When he dances he has peculiar motions and figures of his own and gets into trances. The other boys try to make fun of him. He is the leader of the peyote cult, here." It seems that the pueblo is divided into two camps about the peyote, the old men being set against it as usual.

Well, I don't know what to think of it. Has Tony sent him to me? It looks hardly that way. I am leery of making too much connection with him. That will set the orthodox old men against me. On the other hand I might get more valuable information from him than from the old men. I must look out. He said to me, "Two days ago, before you came, I got a warning. I felt like a wind through my ear and a rumbling noise like water under the ground." His whole appearance is that of a fanatic and a neurotic.

Talking of neurotics, that Lawrence is certainly one. They make a strange outfit he and his wife, an enormous German, exceedingly rational and direct, who looks more like his mother than his wife—and an undescribable Scotch girl, who is deaf, and carries about a box with a radio outfit connected by a tube with her left ear, and whose sister is married to the Maharaja of

49

D.H. Lawrence. *His face is a combination of Tolstoy, G.B. Shaw, and Abraham Lincoln . . .*

Sarawac (an independent kingdom in Borneo, conquered and ruled by an English family). She wears a peaked hat like the Italian brigands, breeches and a long knife stuck in her boot. She is the daughter of a lord, speaks with an exaggerated English accent, looks like an idiot and is very intelligent and completely and utterly independent, with a face that is enough to excite laughter: a long pulled out nose, a receding chin and two sticking-out incisors. Lawrence, it seems, carries her around the world like a talisman. Her name is Miss Bret and they call her "Bret" or "the Bret."

Lawrence is ridiculous as only an Englishman can be ridiculous. His face is a combination of Tolstoy, G. B. Shaw and Abraham Lincoln, very pallid skin, and a semi-bushy semi-goat-like red beard. You expect an enormous body to support that head, but it is only a long, gaunt, raw-boned, awkward succession of ungainly articulations. Undescribable clothes. Checkered trousers stuck in a pair of low cowboy boots, a pleated shirt (soft), a mere ribbon of a black tie dangling down the front, and on his back something of white woolen stuff that is neither a vest nor a coat but is, apparently, of Scotch extraction. To top it all a high, thin, querulous voice.

His mental make up is fully as queer. He has quarrelled with everybody under the sun, and I am not surprised. He is clever, keen, biting, with the sensitiveness of a woman, the aggressiveness of a cock, a bad temper, full of insolence, entirely irrational. His wife, Frieda, is a rock of the ages, immense, a very Germania, sound, solid, with the small ankles and wrists of aristocrats and delicacy of features in spite of superabundances of flesh and squareness of structure. She must be much older than him. He is thirty-eight. She mothers him and adores him and cuffs him. He is absolutely dependent on her, and rages and quarrels with her, and utterly loses his temper. "Pull in your belly, you big bitch,"—this in public—her eyes flash, "Oh! you are such an ass"—

He hates America, violently, virulently, insultingly. His pet abomination is the knightly cow-boy. He hates the whole white race. It is dead, stinking, a loathsome corpse. He has buried it. He digs it up to give it another kick, to shake the rag once more. No use arguing, it's all bunk, bunk, BUNK. Science is bunk, religion is bunk, psychoanalysis is bunk. He rants and rants. He bores me, then. At other times he says things that are deep and keen and delightful. Altogether a very sick fellow.

Taos — April 14, 1924

Nothing has happened yet. I have followed my plan of keeping very quiet. I put the time to profit by staying in my room for three or four days (how many exactly? I don't remember) and writing that story I have had in my mind since last year. At last it is finished and I feel better. I think it is very good, although I can't imagine it's interesting to anyone else but myself. It is a fantastic production of my own dreaming and has neither tail nor head as they say in French.

Tomorrow I will start going to the pueblo. I have had many invitations from several Indians. One of them is Tony's uncle. He is still sore at Tony because he married a white woman. They say he is a very influential member of the council, and a very crabbed old man. "You'll never get a thing out of *him*," says Tony, "he is the kind that can lead you all around the place and ask you and find out all they want and never tell you anything." That old man came to my room, day before yesterday, and spent four hours there. We talked about many things. I flattered his vanity, but he saw through it and smiled. He was friendly, though. "You are the first white man I have heard talk that way. You know many things. White men don't know anything. Yet, it's all in their books. But they have forgotten what it means. I would like to speak to you, but my mouth is sealed. I have never opened my heart to a white man. Not even to other Indians of other places. They have their things and we have our things." I impressed upon him that I wanted those things for the good of humanity (I think that is the only way to impress them. It is what I want to do—perhaps I am a fool—but anyway that is my illusion. And I think I can tell them the truth and they will understand it, in their own way)—and that they would have to tell me, sooner or later, if the spirits in their hearts commanded them to do so. He said I could learn words, not in the pueblo, but here, there were plenty of young Indians who wanted money, and they would tell me words, just words and names of things, but nothing of what is secret. I said I would also like to learn the language, apart from the other thing, but I would not do it that way, only if the old man gave me full consent. Maybe my method of procedure is all wrong, and I'll get left out in the cold. But now I have started that way, I must keep on.

Meanwhile, another caricature has arrived. A woman they call Nina. She has a face like a horse, bobbed hair, is about forty-five, and has just been analyzed by Brill. She came here to finish divorcing her second husband, some kind of a horrible individual, a one-armed loafing uneducated woodsman she married to copy Mabel's act. And he proceeded to carouse with her money and procreate a child with some wench. Well, she came the other day, saw him the next, talked with him for five hours, forgave him, took him back, slept with him that night, gave him

53

money, and now he is reeling drunk around the village. Rather a feeble-minded performance.

Maybe it's a wig.

And Ida Rauch turned up here, too. She lives in Santa Fe, with the man she married after divorcing Max Eastman. As nervous, clever, as ever.

All these people rather bore me. They can't think straight and splash about in shallow intellectual waters, with a good deal of shrieking, but without ever going deep. As Tony (who goes bravely to sleep in his arm chair every evening) said to me, "They talk and talk and talk. And the more they talk, the harder I sleep. It means just nothing at all, all they say."

Lawrence is sore at me. He claims he loves me and wants to save me from the destruction of my hyperintellectualism which is nothing but bunk, bunk, BUNK. The truth is that he is in the habit of bullying people in argument, and *not* in the habit of meeting with the rock wall of insolent contempt I raised between us when he started to rant foolishly. When he behaves he can be very charming. And he tells stories wonderfully well. But he gives a creepy feeling of being too much an old woman, a quarrelling old woman.

Mabel's establishment is just simply immense. Ida Rauch said something extremely picturesque and just of her, "Mabel fantasies herself as a little girl giving a party." She must have oodles of money. And in a subtle way she manages to impose her will on everyone. I am careful to let her run me—at least her just share of it. Besides, I like her. She has charm and is very kind and generous. But she has very little discrimination, either about people or things. (By the way, she is absolutely, idiotically, crazy about you. You are some wonderful mother woman, with a mysterious charm and an amazing wonderful child. Poor little solemn Alvar and his look like an alderman, has become a philosopher to be. She is curiously sentimental in spots. She cannot idealize me at so short a range—so she idealizes you.) She dresses like a little girl, in pinks and ribbons, and by God, in spite of her forty-five years, she does look the part and cute, not even ridiculous. The immense house, or rather succession, procession of houses, are chuck full of the worst amoncellement of beautiful and rare things, Chinese, old Europe, Hindoo, Japanese, Indian, helter-skelter just like a curiosity shop. Of course it kills the place, which is all of the pueblo type, or old Spanish type, bare walls of adobe and mud-plaster, with bare rounded beams, just the peeled trunks of trees.

It makes me laugh. Here they are, talking about the grandeur of the landscape, so immense and bare. And straightaway they proceed to put frills and laces on it with their chatter, their bric-a-brac, their picnics, their rushing about on horseback rides, gossiping, painting, talking of the wonderful Indian and in their heart laughing at his superstition—and every last one of them believes in chiropractics!

Well, tomorrow, I will begin to move. Maybe I will get nothing. At least not this time, perhaps next year, my crop will have sprouted.

I can't stay much longer. I must soon hit the trail back. I plan to walk back. The railroad fare is too much. I think I will get rides nearly all the way. I ought to make it in a couple of weeks or ten days.

Things continue to be dull. I had a talk with the old man, Tony's uncle, and he started to tell me some things, most of which I already knew, being similar to the culture of other Pueblos, but one or two were new to me. However, he broke off suddenly and said, "I am afraid of you. I think you are a white man. You go back home to California. You come back again, I think, maybe I tell you more then." I have also made a good friend of that young boy who was Clarence's special friend. I explained who I was to him. It will be duly repeated to the old men.

I find that Tony has been banished from all ceremonies for having married a white woman, and this hangs over him like a black cloud.

Well, antagonism to the whites has certainly reached its acme in this pueblo. No white man is ever allowed to spend even one night in the pueblo.

So that I completely despair of ever obtaining any mythology—at least this year, inasmuch as the time for my leaving approaches. The whole bunch, Tony, Mabel, the Lawrences and the talisman English girl are going to see a dance that is to take place in Santo Domingo, one of the pueblos that Tony and I came thru on our way here—we spent one night there. As they are going in the machine—two days from here—this will be a fine chance for me to cover the first lap of my trip.

Perhaps I will come back next year, and the seeds I have so carefully sown will have begun to grow, and the Indians less suspicious. I have been so careful and quiet.

Mabel's house is not really a good place to carry on operations from. The Indians are, I think, somewhat antagonistic. The marriage was very much disapproved of. Some of the many guests she has are dabbling in peyote. One woman lives with an Indian who has besides a wife in the pueblo. It's a queer mix-up of artists and would-be artists and Indians and peyote cult and chiropractics and new thought. I must say that Mabel herself is against peyote and has made Tony abandon it—and she has broken relations with that other woman. But I can see that all of this makes the old man suspicious of any guest of hers.

But I do agree with P. L. Faye. Pueblo psychology is a nasty one—too full of intrigue, lying, suspicion, gossip—too far-removed from the big open life. These Indians are petrified in an attitude of submissive obedience to a labyrinth of secret rules and orders. They have no individualities at all, not a shred of initiative. The Navajos and Apaches preyed on them too long. Too long they have been penned in their pueblos like sheep in a pen, distilling the intricate pattern of religious symbolism. I long to breathe freely with my California Indians and their oneness with nature. They don't need so many ceremonies to understand the life of the world in the trees, in the rivers, in the rocks.

1924

Taos — Easter Sunday

The pueblo is very sad and all upset. Yesterday, the Commissioner of Indian Affairs, Burke, came thru here on a tour of inspection and told the Indians that they must put a stop to their ceremonies.

What a stupidly cruel thing to do.

It is hard to keep calm and not to believe as all the hot heads in the Indian Defense Association do that the Government is willfully trying to kill off the Indian and thus put an end to the too onerous and too bothersome trust.

For my part I don't believe it. I think it is just another case of American bullying, of the hundred percent variety, that combined with the traditional ignorance of the Bureau of Indian Affairs in all that is Indian. I will not do them the honor of believing them capable of understanding that to take away his religious ceremonies from the Indian is to take away his heart, and leave him a corpse, ready for quick disintegration.

It is just plain stupid, brutal, arrogant, Nordic superiority.

But there is some meanness, too, in this case. For here is what Burke did. We happen to know that on his way here he stopped at Santa Fe and had a luncheon love-feast with the group of the Indian Defense Association, that bunch of artists, reformers and other "ists," who have made things pretty hot recently about the Indian lands question, the Bur-Suni bill, etc. Well, he had his love-feast with them. Then he came here in a machine, assembled the old men in the school house and delivered his ukase and then sped on to another pueblo. There was no white man there, no witness at all, only the old men of the pueblo. He told them that they must stop their ceremonies and all that nonsense and give their energy to ploughing. And the boys who are in retreat preparatory to initiation must be sent to school immediately. And they must discourage all those artists and fellows with long hair (the old man who reported all this to me, understood, "long beards," and I couldn't imagine what he meant for a long time), discourage all those people from coming to the pueblo and don't listen to them. It is their interest to keep the Indian ignorant and unprogressive. They make their money out of him.

So the pueblo is terribly upset. How are the initiation young men ever going to learn all the intricacies of the teachings about life and the world and what a good Indian must be like, if they are taken away from the old men and sent to school?

The consternation in the pueblo is profound. Everybody is depressed. The old men are holding council upon council. There is no more fight in these Indians. They are scared stiff. You can bluff them easily.

I spent the afternoon writing an article. I believe the only thing to do is publicity. That's the great weapon in America. There is also another method. I think the scientists could band themselves together and work from the inside, from the top, thru the influence of influential circles in Washington. There must be in Washington some honest people with influence. I think that perhaps the best program is to direct all efforts towards taking the Bureau of Indian Affairs out of politics and amalgamating it with the Bureau of American Ethnology.

Can't we get Boas and Elsie and Wissler, Kroeber, Lowie, Goddard, et al. to do something? I think the danger is much greater than they realize.

Taos. Easter Sunday. later

Tony just came back from the pueblo. He said: "The old men she is all feeling very bad. She is shut up in his room crying, all of them. She say now we know we are finish this time."

It is all very sad. More things are coming to the light, that transpired at that meeting where there were no white witnesses. It appears that Burke (or however you spell his name—I don't know whether I have it right; anyhow he is the Indian Commissioner)—it appears he was pretty rough and dictatorial. One Indian who speaks English fairly well was telling us all this morning, "He don't let us talk at all. He pace up and down like wild animal, just keep shouting. This man here (pointing to an old man who also came along with the delegation sent to Mabel) he want to answer. But Mr. Burke he tell him to shut up. I don't want to hear what you have to say. You have nothing to say. You do what I tell you. And then he leave without even shaking hands, just like that. I don't think that good way to talk. He talk to us like slaves but I don't think we are slaves."

I rather think myself that Burke has made the wrong move. Evidently he has been exasperated by the interference of artists, anthropologists, Indian welfare workers and other "fellows with long beards." But everybody is up in arms, now. There have been dissensions in the ranks of the Indian Welfare Association or whatever the name of the thing is, and bitter feeling, each side saying that's not the way to help the Indian, my way is better. But now everybody is joining hands to face the common enemy: the Indian Bureau. The plan seems to be to concentrate on getting the Bureau out of politics and subordinating it to the Bureau of American Ethnology.

They want me because I am an anthropologist to get the scientists together, Boas and Elsie Parsons and Kroeber and the rest as I said this morning. But what can I do? I am a nobody. And besides I don't believe the anthropologists want to be bothered. I don't know what to do. Show this to Lowie and ask him if he will do something. His voice will carry much. . . .

The rest of the letter was lost.

It seems that the Commissioner of Indian Affairs, Burke, that Jaime talks of was a well known and a controversial figure at the time, and a perfect example of the kind of person who was handling Indian affairs and the ideas they had.

Elected in 1898 to the House of Representatives from South Dakota, he served on the House Committee on Indian Affairs, and there wrote legislation designed to protect Indians during the twenty-five-year probationary period before they were to be granted citizenship. It provided, among other things, that they should not be given title to their land allotments until they were judged competent.

He was appointed Commissioner of Indian Affairs under President Harding, at a time when the policies of the bureau were being reexamined, and the nineteenth-century policy of assimilation was being challenged by those who thought that it ought to be abandoned in favor of a policy of greater respect for the rights of the Indians, rights to preserve their culture and their religious practices. Burke's temperament seems to have led him to compromise at one time, and take unpopular stands at another.

Burke was very much interested in improving Indian education and health, both of which were very poor. A great many Indian children never went to school at all, for lack of any. When education was made compulsory for Indian children, in 1920, boarding schools were set up, and the children sent away from their families and forbidden to speak their native languages, something which Indian defenders felt would lead to the destruction of the Indian culture.

Burke believed, like most of his contemporaries, that the Indians were superstitious and backward, and he did all that he could to help those working to convert them to Christianity. Before the 1920s few people considered the right of Indians to practice their own religion. Burke even went so far as to try to limit the duration of Indian dances, and to censor parts of the ceremonials that he considered immoral. In 1923 he forbade persons under thirty from even attending the dances!

Burke considered that the Indians spent too much time on the ceremonials to the detriment of their farms and livestock, and along with many others who truly had the welfare of the Indians at heart, he felt that their only hope of a future lay in assimilation. These attitudes of course ran headlong into the defense of the Indians led by Mabel, Collier, and others. The conflict reached its peak on this occasion when Burke confronted the elders of the Taos tribe and ordered them to put back in school the two boys who had been taken out for an eighteen-month period of religious training.

There were clashes of the same kind in Jemez and Zuñi pueblos, and after two years of conflict a compromise was reached whereby Indian children were excused from school who were certified as candidates for religious training.

Burke seems to have tried, in general, to improve the handling of Indian lands and their resources, but he was not even successful there. In the end his honesty was called in question, and, attacked on the one side by the establishment in Indian policy, and on the other by Collier and the defenders of the Indians, he was driven to resign in March of 1929.

I don't know anything about Jaime's return trip to Berkeley except that he evidently didn't get enough rides after all because he had to take the train.

He soon must have been in correspondence with Mabel, and she must have written that Tony would like a letter himself, because Jaime wrote Tony, and told him about getting a deer hide for his uncle.

June 1924

So, you want me to write "straight to you," Tony. But that is quite unnecessary—you know what my thoughts are, the deep ones, those deep in my heart. Even at a distance of a thousand miles you must feel my friendship. When you see me again, we will just keep on, as if it were only the morrow. I am not *all* coyote, my big brother Bear. My heart is deep, too—it is quite different from my head. You could lock your "box" against me, but not your heart. That's enough for me and I can wait until I see you again.

And as for the little news, there are not much. I am pretty busy helping Nancy or working on the grammars of my Mexican languages. And there is always a lot of friends passing through our house.

I took a short trip to my ranch a little while ago and got a deer. I skinned it carefully. I am going to pack it and send it to you as a present for your uncle. I like him. I also saved the sinews of the back muscles, and the long tendons of the leg.

I have learned to drive the car very well, so next year we will all have a fine trip together.

I have made two drums with old kegs and rawhide. One of them is quite large (out of a lime barrel). It gives a fine booming deep note.

My friend Paul-Louis Faye is here. He is the man I told you about, who lives with a Navajo sometimes. He is as much an Indian as we are. We are all happy together.

Alvar is growing very fast. He is very healthy. He laughs all the time.

Jaime obviously enjoyed showing Tony and his uncle that he knew how to skin a deer and save the tendons Indian fashion. And he was certainly trying to gain favor; he was still planning to go back and work the Taos language and learn something about the religion.

In this next letter, to Cary, he went into Indian psychology from a Jungian viewpoint.

Berkeley. July 10, 1924

Lissen! if we keep on not writing each other more frequently than we have been doing this spring we shall soon lose sight of one another completely. I daresay you have been as busy as I have, with that material of Jung's. I never spoke to you about that: one of the ten million things that I have been accumulating—well, when I read your letter, the one in which you announced it, and you warned me not to tell anyone, and you added that you ought not to tell me, but you knew I *would feel so proud of you*—well, I began to cry. I knew then that I was really back in your heart.

I wonder if the Goodriches are back already. They will tell me all the news. That is if I find time to go down there. Oh I guess I *will* find the time. I am so curious to know. Just think, I don't know at all how they fared or anything. I have not had a word of you,—I daresay that, too, kept you pretty busy.

But, let's see, first of all I am going to try to catch up on my side, and give you an account of my life this spring.

I don't know whether you ever understood how I happened to go on that trip to Taos, so suddenly. It was this way: I was absolutely worn out by the building of the house. Now Nancy was in it, with the baby, everything was all right, and I just naturally slumped. I had kept myself pitched beyond normal endurance because of the necessity—and when the necessity withdrew, I simply slumped like a limp rag. So when Tony said: "I am going next Saturday, you come along"—I went. I thought the change would do me good—and it did. Only it set me back about a month in my linguistic work and in my correspondence. And ever since I came back I have been trying to catch up and I have not yet.

It is very annoying—for instance I meant to write for Jung a resumé of my impressions anent the psychological make up of the Pueblo Indians. And I haven't done it yet.

One of the things that puzzle me is: is there at that stage of culture a division into the two types of extraverts and introverts? Sometimes I am inclined to think that there isn't—or rather that the flow of the psychological energy is pretty evenly divided in each individual Indian. I think that very often, they deliberately turn the tap of nature, as it were, and let the elements flow in. At other times they are busy, doing some kind of craft work, bead work, leather work, and then their minds do not work, or rather are not attuned to nature, they just do the work, intent on the work.

Is there a division into the four functions? There again I would say that there is, but that each individual is pretty well balanced. That's what puzzles so many anthropologists and other people who try to understand the Indians. I think it is entirely wrong to say like Levy-Brühl that the Indian mind is pre-logical only. It is logical just as often as it is irrational, I should say. It is we of the post-Renaissance culture, who are one-sided, logical, rational to the exclusion of the irrational. So when Levy-Brühl finds so many examples of use of non-logical functioning he is led to believe that it is always that way. Because for Levy-Brühl the two, that is the rational and the irrational are mutually exclusive, cannot exist side by side. One must precede the other, chronologically. The irreconcilability between the two would be intolerable to Levy-Brühl and all other scientists. But it is not so to the Indian.

As to feeling and sensation, I would say that Indians do not find it necessary to sacrifice either of the two to any other, the way we do.

In short, as I see it, there is no differentiation, or rather, there is differentiation but each man carries the whole burden equally balanced. Only, as a whole, the psychological level is lower,—by that I mean that it flows at a slower rate than with us. It is more diffuse, more somnolent, less conscious. Perhaps it was necessary, in order to obtain that keener degree, that intenser psychic life, to destroy the balance and develop each function separately.

Now please read this to Jung and favor me with some criticism. Tell me if I am on the right road, or whether what I suggest is impossible.

Interrupted . . . July 17

Well, to come back to the trip to Taos. Of course I got a great deal out of it, for my own personal use—that is I immersed myself deeper yet into the Indian view point—and I also laid the basis for many friendships—another time if I go back there I will have a much better chance to obtain information. But of direct, material information I got none this time. It had been my intention, if I were able to get something of tangible value, to draw on the Jung fund (which is still intact) to help defray my expenses—altho these did not amount to much as I was a guest of the Luhans most of the time, I only had to pay for the return trip. But I didn't get anything that would justify spending that money—and the trip was undertaken as a private recreation not a field-trip. So I have still the five hundred, and my plans are the same to go to the Achumawi this winter.

After I came back from Taos, I plunged into my Zapotek linguistic work, to make up for lost time. It is going to be a monumental piece of work when it is finished. The pity of it is that nobody will ever read it, probably. Probably it will never be published. They seem to have less money than ever in Mexico. I keep sending some chapters of the grammar to Gamio, from time to time, as I finish them. You see I am writing a comparative grammar of seven languages at once—seven languages that are related, but not more closely than say Sanskrit, Spanish, English, Russian, Irish, Lithuanian and Greek. So that I have to do by my lonely all the work that it took many scholars to do in the Indo-European field. It's a tremendous job. Sometimes it discourages me a little to think that my manuscript will probably be buried in a drawer in Mexico City. Yet, I have made some really important discoveries—of a general nature in the mechanism of language. But after all I work mainly for the fun of creating. —And it is also a secret pleasure to receive the notes of acknowledgment from Gamio. I can see he is rather flabbergasted at the amount of material I gathered in Mexico. He is very friendly and keeps saying that he hopes things are going to take a better turn financially—but, what's the difference—I will not work under the old conditions. . . .

The Taos Papers

Part Two

The Second Trip

Some time in May or June of 1924 Jaime must have received a letter from Mabel inviting him and Nancy to come to Taos and visit again. This time Lawrence would not be there. Jaime wrote her:

June 1924

Your letter just came. Paul-Louis Faye said "Let's all go. I have deferred my trip long enough. There are several families of Navajo that I want to see in Arizona. Then we will all go to Taos which I have never seen." Nancy demurred. What about the baby's food. She said, "You two boys go." But I refused to leave her alone again.

So here we are, starting in a few days, with our Haynes and his Ford.

She is brave to take Alvar. But I think it can be managed. She needs a trip, very much, indeed.

We will drop you postals on the way. Gosh! it's going to be fun!

Jaime and Alvar. *America's Oldest Car.*

I don't think in fact that Paul-Louis Faye went. There are no pictures of him among the snapshots of the trip. But Jaime and Nancy did indeed drive down in their car, an ancient Haynes convertible coupe, which they called after the company's motto, America's Oldest Car. It took a month to get there.

They stayed in Tony's own little house on the reservation, a short way from the Lodge. There is no diary of this trip, that I know of, but there are a few typewritten sheets along with the diary of the first trip that must have been written at this time.

Turtle Old Man was Jaime's term for Tony's uncle.

Last evening I went to the pueblo. I wanted to see my friend Turtle Old Man. I sat on the step of his house to wait for him. After awhile a woman passed by. She spoke a few words "I think he is gone somewhere . . . I don't know . . . maybe he come back pretty soon." After a few moments she passed by again, and said some other meaningless thing. I noticed her: tall, sinewy for an Indian woman, very high cheek bones and oblique eyes with strange heavy dormant eyelids. Very soon she passed again in front of me. She had a pair of scissors in her hand.

"I take those scissors back to my mother-in-law. I borrow them. You come and talk to me in her house."

I went with her. We went up a ladder, over a flat roof, through a low door, into the usual bare, white-washed clean sort of pueblo room. They are like monk's cells these Indian dwellings. She introduced me to her father-in-law and her mother-in-law. They smiled. They soon were bored with the conversation in English, which they do not speak. The young woman was a great talker. We spoke of the usual topics. Of how the people had just come down from the mountain after celebrating the autumn festival. How they danced and held religious ceremonies for several days. How the whites did not understand the Indian ways, and wanted to destroy the Indian ways.

"What are you?" she said. "Are you an Indian or a white man? You don't dress like a white man. You know lots of Indian ways. Do you believe as we do?"

The woman was beginning to interest me. Something in her wild, unrestrained, so unlike the ordinary Pueblo Indian who is passive, secretive, suspicious—you have to drag things out of him, and always he tries to hide his thoughts, forever afraid of criticism and the gossip of his fellow Indians of the pueblo, afraid that the old men of the council will reprimand him for "giving away secrets to white people," for "selling ceremonies"; the Pueblo Indian is not a man, he is only a member of his community, afraid of the old men, afraid of the criticism of his neighbours. And such a gossipy place as a pueblo is! Imagine five hundred people living their whole lives, packed on a few acres of ground, where the adobe houses are built one atop the other, and everyone on the house tops spying on everybody else. There is absolutely no privacy, ever. Oh give me my Achumawi roaming over their plain, camping at a spring.

Well, to return to this woman of the heavy lids, there was something unrestrained and frank and unbridled about her. So we talked about things, of the new peyote cult and its evil influence, of religion, of water. I said: "You have power, I think."

"Yes," she answered, "I have. How do you know? My people are afraid of me. My power is of my dreams, that's where my power is. But I don't know how to use it. I don't know what to do with it. When my power comes, then I feel weak. And I feel bad, too, and I am cross. I am mean to everybody, anyone who comes near me I am cross to them, a child, a woman, a man, anyone. My husband comes home and right away he feels it and he don't speak to me, he lie down. I stay like that for a week, maybe more, maybe a month, then it's all over. I had attacks when I was a child (and here she described typical epilepsy), since I was thirteen until I got married. But not anymore since

Pueblo mother and son.

then. I think my child took it away from me. He is a strange child, he is six now. When he was five years old, he was out gathering pine-nuts with his grandmother and he began to say foolish things in play; he said to her: 'You see that crack in the ground, that's where I came from.'

" 'What foolish thing is that you say,' my mother told him. 'How can you have been below the ground?'

" 'Yes, I was down there,' he said. 'There was another place just like here, with people and horses and mountains and everything. I lived down there. Then I got ready, I climbed a rope for a long time, I climbed and climbed along that rope. Then I got thru a lot of mud and I was here.'

"After that he began to talk to people, and all the men always try to make him talk, the old men, he is always running around; they say I don't take care of him, but I never can find him; the old men hide him from me when I look for him, they want to make him talk. They say he has a strange power. He tells them his father in that other place kept sheep, and he hired two boys to herd the sheep. One his name was T'elesene, and the other his name Sunlesene, he just made up those names himself. It doesn't mean anything in our language. He make up all sorts of stories like that. He is a strange boy."

It was getting near sunset. "I guess I go now," she said, "we talked long enough, you come and see me again. I wanted to talk to you. I just had to. I saw you last time you came to the pueblo with your wife and your baby. I make up my mind I want to know you. Well, goodbye, maybe the old man, your friend, he is back now. Are you going to stay with him tonight?"

"Maybe, I don't know, maybe he won't let me."

"He can if he wants to, the old men don't allow any stranger to stay at night in the pueblo but he is an old man himself, one of the oldest men, they all listen to him, and he can do as he pleases. He can keep you in his house, if he likes."

But Turtle Old Man was not back.

74

Monday morning.

An Indian was wandering around here yesterday afternoon, doing something to the ditches. I think he is working for one of the neighbors. We entered into conversation. For a while he seemed willing to talk. To help getting him to drop his defence, and show him my sympathy with the Indian point of view, I told him some of the things I have already learned. He listened for awhile, then he got into rage.

"Who told you all these things? I know who it is, it's your friend Turtle Old Man, and Tony Luhan, yes, yes, I am sure of it, damn fool old men, they are the first ones to go and tell all our things, all our Indian things; our things, our religion, our prayers are for us, not for your nation, our language we must keep for ourselves, I don't want you to learn it, and I'll see that you don't learn another thing, too. I'll tell them, I'll tell the people who told you, damn fool old men!" and he stalked off muttering and scowling.

I have met here a white man, intelligent, a painter, or rather was one and gave it up, now keeps a curio store. Well, he was practically raised here and he seems to know the Indians pretty well, also to have a good realization of the value of Indian culture, so his point of view counts.

He says: "I remember twenty years ago—you could get all the information you wanted from the Indians, all of them were ready to help you, but after awhile they saw some of the things that have been published, in magazines, books and the like, about Indians, and they got the notion that white men had made a lot of money out of it, that they had made millions out of the Indians; they got the notion that everything Indian was very valuable and they said: 'The whites have made lots of money out of us, but they have given us nothing, we are just as poor as before, now we must never tell them anything any more.' "

I don't know whether he is right or not. I rather think he is. These Indians are so different from our California Indians. Over there they have not been spoiled by the tourist element. Of course they have none of the picturesque, which is what attracts, here, the tourist element, and I mean not only here in Taos, but all over the "South-west." And it applies not only to the typical Pueblos, but also to the nomadic tribes like the Navajo. Whether the Navajo have taken their rather well developed artistic sense from the Pueblos, or from the Spaniards or had it in themselves, or is it the geography that is responsible for it? I don't know.

Anyway, here it is, all over this region of Arizona and New Mexico, a highly developed sense of art, and it is expressed in everything; in the designs of blankets, in ceremonies, in dress, there is color, there is form, there is pattern. All of the psychological stuff, I mean that mess of material that comes from all the outer world and is there cooking, par-boiling, simmering in the bottom of their souls, all that stuff here seems to get projected once more into the outer world, in the shape of pattern, of form, of design, in everything, in dancing and in ritual, in weaving, in pottery. —It seems almost as if these people could not stand the existence in their souls of the psychological reflection of the outer biological world . . . something too strong, too powerful, would make you vomit, have to conjure it, to exorcise it, get it out, "fix" it in pattern, in outer form, —there it still lives, it's not dead, it lives for anyone who can understand with the heart, not with the eyes, the pattern on the blanket, or in the ritual, it lives for him, but it is not dangerous any longer.

That's how they impress me, and I think this is true not only of the Pueblos, of the true Pueblos, but also of the Hopi (who live in pueblos also, and have all the culture of the Pueblo, but are Shoshonean by language) and also of the roaming Navajo and Apache who are Athapascan by language.

Now most of this country is the picturesque Grand Canyon type of landscape, chuck full of colour and form, where erosion has produced grotesque monstrous shapes everywhere, where instead of the multitudinous variety of trees, shrubs and hillocks, valleys with woods and streams and boulders—indeed of that nature broken into an infinity of small pieces, there are immense spaces, desert, no trees, no shrubs even, but the result of erosion in stratified rocks, in violent colours, definite lines, many parallels, many perpendiculars, other angles also, but always well defined, a merciless sunlight and sharp shadows from the luminous to utter black. Our artists try to paint it, they can't, they are too subtle, they know their art too well, they see too many colors, too many shades—worse, they try to imitate the Indians but they don't understand *fear*, they are afraid of material dangers, of snarling dogs, of a rushing train, of the flu, of their boss or their wife, but they are not afraid of the spirit that walks silently in the shimmer of the sunlight, and so they can't paint the desert. You can't paint the desert or even talk about it, you can only put it in a blanket design, and the Navajo know the desert better than the rest and their designs are fierce and uncompromising— that's why Lawrence (and Mabel too) don't like Navajo rugs. Lawrence because he is jealous of everything that is wild and untamed and strong. He thinks he has a copyright on it. Mabel both because she is under his influence and because she has identified herself with these Taos Indians, who are the least wild, the most bourgeois of all.

Well, to come back to my sheep, I mean: Is it perhaps that this kind of geography (high plateau, dry, sand, light, etc. etc.) is responsible for the external form, I mean rather for the aspect of the form into which these people had to exorcise, to fixate, to crystallize and externalize their inner feelings? I don't think much of the sort of explanation that is always trying to reduce psychology to a question of climate and economics. But that factor must also be remembered.

And now I think of the California Indians. (I speak of the Achumawi especially). Have they externalized their inner feelings? They have no pottery, no blankets, no houses, nothing to put pattern into, not even dances or ceremonials. They go around naked (I paint them as they were before '49); all they have is a piece of flint for a knife and a bow and arrows. They do not till the soil. They just collect what the soil grows: roots, bulbs, acorns, pine-nuts—and whatever is an animal, from worms to bears—they eat anything, and almost raw. Why, they are hardly differentiated from the trees and the brushes and the deer and the antelope and the rain and the snow and everything that is Nature. Where is the line of demarcation between a juniper tree and an Achumawi Indian? What's the difference? Not much. But there is a hell of a lot of difference between a Taos Indian and the corn he has planted and raised! He already controls nature (or tries to control it)—he is no longer nature itself, like the Achumawi Indian. The Achumawi (especially he who is more or less of a "doctor," who has "power") is in constant relation with the living part, the "spirit" part of every tree, every rock, every cloud, every shrub, every toad, and every deer who lives around. I doubt very much whether they have any image inside of them, in their souls, I mean. So he is afraid of them and of their possible malignancy (just as he is afraid of every other Achumawi Indian, or any other Indian), he is afraid of them, and tries to keep them well disposed and on good terms of intercourse, he even feels them as rather weird and dangerous and too powerful (like electricity with us); but he is not so damn scared, blue scared of them and their inside image (maybe just because he has no inside image) that he must needs exorcise them out into objective reality. The Pueblo Indian takes everything that is aweful, terrible, powerful in nature, Sun, Moon, Earth, pollen and flower, and he corrals it into a ceremony, or a pattern, now he doesn't have to deal with it anymore at every moment of his life, like the Achumawi, now he can become a gentleman, safe and sane.

It seems that Nancy was right when she had said that on a second trip Jaime would be an old friend, and have the confidence of the Indians. The old men evidently did let him study the language, and they must even have let him get some information about the religion. But he never published anything on the religion, so there is no way of knowing.

Just before he left Taos Jaime wrote Edward Sapir about getting down the Taos language. Jaime had first written Sapir several years before, after having read his book, *Language*.

Jaime wrote on a card:

> One more language with tones. Got it in fine shape.
> I am going home now to write it up. Will send you a copy.
>
> Angulo
> Taos, Sep't. 30, 1924

All I know about their trip back is what Nancy wrote Mabel the next spring—that and that they bought a Ford Touring Car in Taos, so they didn't return in America's Oldest Car.

1925

Dear Mabel,

You have by now left Taos as far behind as we, and I suppose are wrestling already with New York, and crowds, and Brill—and are all cross feeling etc. taking shape as monsters and hallucinations? I often wonder how you are getting on—and Tony. Jaime is slaving over Taos, getting it into form rapidly. Hardly dances any more at all, and scowls when guests arrive. It is a curious and a complex language.

Nancy and Alvar. *They stayed in Tony's own little house on the reservation, a short way from the Lodge.*

What a trip we had! We stayed with Tony's Mexican friend the first night, then camped a few—little cold—one morning a slim little icicle hung from the desert bag. We all three had colds. Then we reached Flagstaff, long past midnight in a terrific storm—frightful piece of road, mainly detours, and we had to stop for tires twice! From then on we drove practically night and day. Reached here Saturday noon—eight-day trip. The garden is lovely—all sorts of gay flowers and foliage tangled into the most charming designs—the profession Jaime *really* should have followed is that of gardener. But of course it is all an inclined plane, and I miss very much being able to wander about on the flat and sit out in it to read or sew. Those were lovely weeks in your Taos garden. Alvar is growing very big and red-cheeked and masterful and eats spinach and prune puree.

There is a young friend of ours here who does a lot of writing—magazine work, publicity and so on. He has been reading some of Jaime's Indian stuff, and wants to collaborate with him— that is, do over some of his material, giving it more form, explaining things that J. assumes are known—and try again to put it across. Maybe he can do it—maybe the project will be a rank mongrel. But he is wondering about photographs—if anything does come of it, do you suppose it would be possible to get some from anyone in Taos that could be had with due acknowledgment. Write some day and tell us all your news. Love to Tony.

Nancy

I have no idea who it was that was trying to collaborate with Jaime, or if anything came of it.

About a month after getting back, Jaime wrote his sister:

Dearest sister,

I just got your letter and I am going to start a new method—which is to answer you right away without even stopping for anything—that's the way you never answer letters, you say to yourself: I will wait until this evening and then I will write a real nice letter——evening comes and you are too tired and sleepy, and you go to bed, then the next day it's the same thing, and the day after that the same again, and soon a month has passed, and then two months, and six months which is half-a-year! and then you say, how in the hell am I going to explain all that has happened and why it is that I am here in Guatemala instead of Berkeley. Here, don't jump and look at the post-mark, this letter is from Berkeley all right. But, if you hear that I am in Guatemala next, don't be surprised, that's all. I may get a job there for the Government, kind of official anthropologist-in-chief, or something like that—anyhow the pay is pretty good: $300 a month. However I am not yet sure of it.

Well, here we have been back from Taos just about a month, and I haven't even started wading into the pile of letters I must answer, and letters to write, and patati and patata. I have pushed everything aside in desperation, to see if I can't write the grammar of that language, finish it, send it to New York, and be done with it. You see, I scooped quite a thing when I got that Taos language. Taos has always been a pueblo of peculiarly secretive Indians. Nobody has ever been able to get any information from them as to their customs, their religion, or their language. They hate white men with a bitter hatred. However, they finally took us in, Nance, Alvar and myself. Alvar was a great favourite from the first, and even got an Indian name bestowed on him: pehluhliina which means Big Deer, in other words the big buck who is boss of the herd and walks in the lead along the trails.

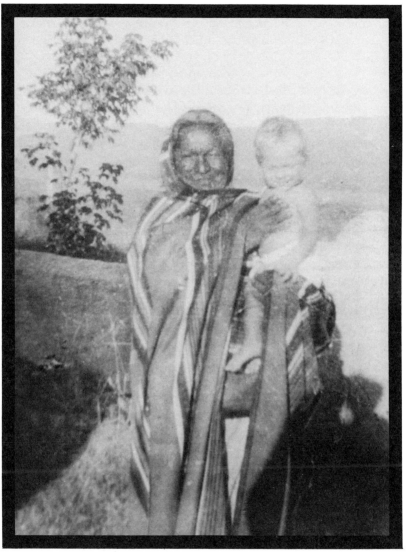

Pehluhliina and friend. *Alvar was a great favorite from the first, and even got an Indian name bestowed on him . . .*

And by all appearances Alvar is going to be that some day, if he continues on the present system of raging good health, sound sleep, and voracious appetite. I bet father would be crazy about him.

You know, we went there in an automobile. About 1500 miles, and back. We had to cross the aweful desert of the Mojave, in southern California. You can feel Death stalking abroad there in the full light of day. Sand, sand, sand, and in the distance tortured mountains, bare and naked, clear-cut in the dancing light. You dream of valleys beyond, hollows filled with heat and noon, and a gold hunter crazed with thirst and visions. Hot, hot, golly it was hot, almost enough to warm me—just imagine, the whole thing is some hundred feet below sea level. Nance was limp with the heat. The Culipan (that's Alvar—one of his titles) he didn't mind it. We had fixed a sort of throne of blankets at the back of the car, and there he sat on high, full wind in the face, shouting his joy or yelling his hunger, proving to all the world that his noble father was right when he said to his doubtful mother, oh! never mind what the doctors say and all the wise people, and the right kind of milk, and patati and patata. We took a crate-full of condensed milk along with us, and we had plenty of dirt along, and sometimes he looked like a nigger baby, and he was hugged by many an Indian woman whose children were full of lice, . . and there he is in the next room, 9 months old, never been sick one day, with his eyes as blue as mine, a worse temper, and a laughter that promises to be as resonant and as irrepressible as his grandmother's, Isabel. . . .

Well I must go back to my darling Taos language, where to say: "my ranch" you have to say: for-me-it-is-plowed-that-which.

Good bye, darling, follow my good example, sit down when you get this, and write. That way, we won't get in arrears again.

And listen, I haven't written to Cary for I don't know how

long, and goodness knows how much longer it will be before I do so. Therefore, would you mind sending this on to her?

J.

Pura did not send the letter on to Cary, but kept it, along with what appear to be all the letters Jaime ever sent his father or her—until her death.

Jaime returned once more to Taos, for a few days only, around New Year, 1925. He went at the invitation of Jung, and he describes the trip in this letter sent to Mabel, who was in New York being analyzed. Here he clearly states his attitude toward the value of Indian culture to the white person.

2815 Buena Vista Way
Berkeley
January 16, 1925

These were two very sweet letters you sent us. We should have answered long ago, but you know how it is with us and no servants, and all the spare time we can scrape devoted religiously to writing up the grammar of the Taos language. We are collaborating on it, N. and I.

Well, by this time you must have heard from Tony an account of my suddenly appearing in Taos with Jung. It was all very sudden. It seems that he decided out of a clear sky to cross over to America for the sake of a little vacation on the steamer. Then the first thing I knew there was a telegram asking me to come and meet him at the Grand Canyon "no expense to you." I recognised the generous hand of Mr. Porter (of Chicago). The telegram mentioned the possibility of visiting an Indian Pueblo.

Taos Indians, one of whom is possibly Antonio Mirabal (Mountain Lake).

You can imagine my excitement. I made up my mind that I would kidnap him if necessary and take him to Taos. It was quite a fight because his time was so limited, but I finally carried it. And he was not sorry that he went. It was a revelation to him, the whole thing. Of course I had prepared Mountain Lake (Antonio Mirabal). He and Jung made contact immediately and had a long talk on religion. Jung said that I was perfectly right in all that I intuited about their psychological condition. He said that evening "I had the extraordinary sensation that I was talking to an Egyptian priest of the fifteenth century before Christ." The trip was an immense success all around. Jung got a great deal out of it. I got a great deal out of Jung, both about philosophy and about my own work. I needed his confirmation of all the stuff I have been working out by my own lonely self and against all anthropological precedent. And I got Porter and young McCormick interested in the Indian question. They realized my thesis: the white American *must* preserve the Indian, not as a matter of justice or even of brotherly charity, but in order to save his own neck. The European can always tie back to his own mother soil and find therein the spiritual pabulum necessary to life. But the American, overburdened with material culture, is threatened with self-destruction unless he can find some way to tie himself to his own mother soil. The Indian holds that key.

They saw my thesis, and they solemnly promised me that they would not forget it but would use their energy and their influence towards some sort of steady campaign. Maybe they will, maybe they won't. Maybe the dream of my life is on its way!

What news of Clarence? and of Lawrence?

J.

Mountain Lake was the Indian with whom Jaime had studied the Taos language.

Up to this point Jaime had not taken a very active part in the battle for Indian rights, as this letter to Sapir shows.

2815 Buena Vista Way
BERKELEY
Feb. 26, 1925

My dear Sapir

Your good letter came just at the psychological moment to help me over a fit of depression. Do you remember how some years ago, when I was working with the Achumawi, you wrote me an encouraging letter and you said that if I intended to enter the field of American linguistics I would have to arm myself with courage, because I would find it neither remunerative nor leading to fame? I have found neither recognition nor the means of independence, and my stock of courage is almost gone. Of course it is true as my wife says, that I am too haughty and contemptuous of worldly standards. I don't go out enough and hunt for trade. If I don't go out into the world I mustn't expect the world to come knocking at my door. There is the example of that Linguistic Society of America, which you mention in your letter. I did see something about it some time ago, I think an invitation or something like that, but immediately I sneered: "another society for mutual back-patting" and I turned again to my texts. Some time ago a bunch of well meaning people here, even tho they are sentimentalists at heart (and sentimentalizing over the Indian is my bête noire!), started an Indian Defense Association of California. I went to the first two meetings, was bored to death half the time, the other half I was mad as a bull at the patronizing attitude of the damfool whites, and I never went again. Now the thing is well launched and is probably going to help the Indians a great deal and I am not in it. I have always made fun of poor little Espinosa and his tackiness. But Espinosa has won more recognition than I have. All the idiots of the earth seem to be able to find a publisher for their stuff, even a martinet like Spier. Look at that book of Jesperson! And he is the foremost European linguist!

And here I sit with the material of eleven new languages and I can't get a line published. Be a good fellow and try to give me a boost.

Yours as ever

Jaime de Angulo

P.S. You are one of the editors of the *Journal of American Linguistics*. Wouldn't it take a paper like this on Mixe?

By April of 1925 Jaime must have been in correspondence not only with Mountain Lake, but with Collier, the great defender of Indian rights himself, and he seems to have wanted to take a more active part in Indian defense. He wrote:

Berkeley
April 3 [1925]

Dear Collier

In a recent letter Antonio Mirabal says: "Every thing is going alright only the Govt. ask us more land to build more building for the school children. So that set us to trouble among our selfs."

You probably know all about it, but I thought I might as well tell you.

I want to see you. I want to take some active part in the

Indian Defense Association. I am not even a member! I am ashamed of myself! I must get out of my ivory tower and into the seething street, before it is too late!

Jaime de Angulo

By May of 1925 Jaime had interested his good friend Chauncey Goodrich in the Indian cause, and wrote him the following letter giving sources for background material on Indian affairs.

Friday
[May 1925]

Dear Ch.

I have been looking all over the place for some of Collier's literature. I thought I had some of his pamphlets around, but I must have given them all away. I am writing him to send you some.

In the "Handbook" look at the article "agency system," it will put you on the track of other articles. Also "Taos" and "Pueblo."

Read the article on the Yana Indians by Waterman. That is very readable.

The other reprints are probably too dry and scientific and will send you to sleep. I mean those by Kroeber. Yet there is good stuff in them . . . but written up in a desolatingly taste-less manner.

The article by Haeberlin is full of information and typically German scholarly.

The article by Freeland has some interesting passages which I wrote myself . . . ahem!

Finally there is here in this your house a complete set of the Reports of the Bureau of Am. Ethnology, also the Bullet. of the same, also the anthropological publications of the U. of C., also two living anthropologists who are at your service.

If you don't mind sleeping on the floor, you can camp here. I have a good mattress and lots of blankets.

J.

Got the bracelet

In May Jaime had evidently received a letter from Ruth Benedict, Franz Boas' student and at that time his assistant, about the possibility of her doing field work in Taos. Jaime had met Benedict when he passed through New York on his way back from Zurich in 1923.

Berkeley, California
May 19, 1925

My dear Ruth

My Taos stuff is purely linguistic and has no value for folklore.

As for helping you to get an informant, and the way you describe it "if I took him with me to a safely American place" . . . "an informant who would be willing to give tales and ceremonials" . . . oh God! Ruth, you have no idea how much that has hurt me. I don't know how I am going to be able to talk to you about it because I have a sincere affection for you. But do you realize that it is just that sort of thing that kills the Indians? I mean it seriously. It kills them spiritually first, and as in their life the spiritual and the physical element are much more interdependent than in our own stage of culture, they soon die of it physically. They just lie down and die. That's what you anthropologists with your infernal curiosity and your thirst for scientific data bring about.

Don't you understand the psychological value of secrecy at a certain level of culture? Surely you must, but you have probably never connected it with this. You know enough of analytical psychology to know that there are things that must not be brought to the light of day, otherwise they wither and die like uprooted plants.

Have you never lived with Indians, Ruth? I really don't know, that's why I ask you. Is your own interest in primitive religion the result of a deep but unacknowledged mysticism? I wonder. You are connected in my mind very strongly with Edna who is still just as present in my life as she was before she died. That's why I talk in this strange way, because I am afraid to hurt your feelings. If it were Mrs. Parsons I wouldn't give a damn. If I ever find her or any other anthropologist ferreting out secrets in Taos or any other pueblo I will immediately denounce her and her informants to the old men. But I couldn't denounce you, and it will break my heart.

Why do you want to know these things? Of course if you promised that you would never publish the *actual* secrets, I would help you all I can. I would tell you a lot myself about the meaning of the whole thing. It is all right to talk about it in a general way, with certain reservations, the necessary care that must be always used in handling all esoteric knowledge. It is as powerful and dangerous as the lightning. Look at all the harm that raw psychoanalysts do to their patients. . . . But the actual details of ceremonies, that must never be told. They are as much part and parcel of the mind of the believer as the pyramidal cells of his cortex. They belong to him. They belong to the secret society. They have a real, actual meaning and value, as secrets, for the members of the society. You must not rob them. You must not sneak into their house. You wouldn't inveigle my child into telling you the secrets of my home.

Don't you see the meaning of it all? In Europe we can go back to our mother the earth through the spirits of our own ancestors. They inhabit the soil, the trees, the rocks. In America the soil is teeming with the ghosts of Indians. Americans will never find spiritual stability until they learn to recognize the Indians as their *spiritual* ancestors. The Sun-father of Egypt is a living symbol yet in the collective unconscious psychology of every European through actual tangible contact with the unbroken chain of organic culture. Only the Sun-father of the American Indian (an entirely different sort of person from that of Egypt) can ever be a father to the white American. That is the legacy of the Indian. But you would lose it by killing the Indian off before that message has been comprehended by the white Americans. And you kill the Indian as surely by disorganizing his spiritual social life as you do with guns.

Well, I have told you what was in my heart. Perhaps it is all gibberish to you. I would rather you would laugh at it than be hurt.

We start on the first of June, in a kind of prairie schooner built on a Chevrolet truck chassis. We will visit first some of our friends among the Pomo. Then the bulk of the summer among the Achumawis. Then across the desert to Taos. Let's keep in touch. We might have some time together, perhaps even in Taos, although I doubt whether they would allow a white man to live in the pueblo, even with us. I really want to have you with us. I am sure I could give you a certain slant on the real life of the Indians. I am not an anthropologist but I am half an Indian, or more.

Don't forget that Cushing killed Zunyi. Mrs. Parsons is doing her best to kill Santo Domingo, but fortunately the people there are on their guard now.

The "prairie schooner" that Jaime speaks of in his letter was the famous "Auto Blanche," a sort of precursor to the modern-day camper, built on a Chevrolet truck chassis by an Oakland cabinet maker. Made with no thought to weight, and containing, as well as camping equipment, a complete reference library for the field worker, she was far too heavy for her brakes, and quite terrifying on mountain roads.

Jaime and Nancy didn't go to Taos that summer, the reason being, no doubt, that Alvar got dysentery at the Achumawi camp, and they drove him home to the hospital, not at all sure that he would survive. He wasn't back to normal until the spring of 1926.

A few days after writing that letter to Ruth Benedict Jaime sent off his Taos grammar to Sapir, with the following letter:

May 23, 1925

Dear S.

THERE SHE GOES! a terrible hodge-podge of half-finished texts, part of the Introduction, notes for the grammar, the phonology just such as to get your goat, but full of intuitive meat, if you'll admit it, and first of all the Semantic List which is really what I want you to have now. The rest is really all too much helter-skelter, but since I have several copies I might as well send this to you. It might come in handy some time, my house might burn again. But you can see that it will take me all of next winter to put it all in shape. (I am following your suggestion of the Monograph Series, I am going to go after my friends. In fact I know dam well that I will get the necessary money, especially for anything connected with Taos. Young McCormick was there with me last winter.) But I have to re-type the whole blooming thing because I am not satisfied with the phonetic transcription. You see I have been experimenting sort-of.

I have been thinking not only of the anthropologists, but of the Indians, the Taos Indians. There is a possibility of their learning to write the language. I have taken the stand that after all, what my informant felt about spelling that should be my guide (whatever else I might think was true scientific phonetics). But he has learned to accept some things he rejected at first. Most of the texts (by the way, that is only about one-third of my material) are in the first system I tried for Taos; my informant insisted on the Spanish jota for the x sound and he got hopelessly confused by the introduction of the t in the tc sound. Instead he preferred to write it like in English church. For the surd l he first had sl, then hl. Finally, to complicate matters for you I had no Hammond when I wrote the first texts, so I had to resort to several makeshifts like ʉ for ï , and writing the pitch tones with a dot above and below, etc. Well, you'll have to guess at a great many things, but it may be of some use to you . . . and now I must begin packing.

J. de A.

As far as I know Jaime never returned to Taos.

In 1933 Collier was appointed Commissioner of Indian Affairs under Franklin D. Roosevelt.

The Witch

Part Three

The story that Jaime wrote and read aloud at Mabel's house, *The Witch*, was the second of his novelettes, and a sequel of sorts to the first one, *Don Bartolomeo*. Along with *The Reata*, written in the Thirties, and with a completely different set of characters, it relies on Indian religion and custom—and also on a sense of fate or damnation which seems to me not to be Indian at all but completely European.

There are two versions of *The Witch*, this one and a later one in which the female lead is a woman anthropologist. But this is the one which Jaime sent Cary, in carbon, on exactly the same thin yellow paper on which he sent her the carbon of his account of the first visit to Taos. I think they were written there; they are handwritten, and in Berkeley Jaime was already using a typewriter.

The Witch

Here I am "down the Coast" again, the wild Coast, where I was born, the mad Coast that rises, impossibly, sheer out of the sea, in this remote corner of the Ventanas. And yet it does not lie so very far from the civilized world—only two or three days on horseback to Monterey the Old. Why was it never settled by the Spaniards? and why have all the Indians disappeared? Is there a curse on this place? Questions without answer. Why did my ancestor come here to bury some sinister memory? He would better have forgotten in a frenzied modern world than pit himself against the eternal sea with his back to the wall of a mountain, with wilder mountains behind, and no issue but on either side, furtively, through a ribbon of a trail clinging along the mountain wall, dizzily above the gleaming ocean. What a place! Remote, full of another life, moody, now stretched blinking in the sun, warming its ravines and steep rounded slopes, while the far traveling ships hardly move under their sails, way off on the smooth sparkling sea, and the whales, migrating wisely puff their breath suddenly, and a condor bathes in the light—now again shivering in the fog, whipped by the winds when the horses take refuge in the canyons from the blinding driving drizzle, brittle oaks snap their branches, the choir of the pines exalt in lamentations and the tall redwoods hurry like ghosts through the mists.

It was stupid of me to come back, especially now at the beginning of winter. Did I hope to cure one madness by another? She will follow me here, she will come. I can't escape from her. Doesn't she know there is danger? Yes, there is danger, even for a mother. A mother! What do I know of a mother, except a word read in books. And I have seen cows with their calves. The earth also, brooding in summertime. Not this wild thing of grace with the glaucuous eyes, dancing madly thru life. Does she not fear the end, the witch, because she does not grow old? Why did she not throw me into the ocean to keep company to my father. She has dragged me, like a crab, in her wake, a bitter contrast to her dazzling beauty. She might have forgotten me in some studious school, and I would have known no mother but the *intarissable* breasts of knowledge, and the philosophers of old would have been the fathers who blessed me. Why drag the ugly, misshapen crab thru the capitals of Europe, for twenty years of roving, breaking camp with each new lover, disguising life in the harlequin colors of wit, the juggling cleverness of salons. She does not even love me, that's not love. I am sick of it all, sick down to the soles of my feet, sick with shame, sick at twenty. Where is my father, to save me from the abomination that creeps in my belly, that rises and drowns my mind—the nameless thing of horror turns into leaping fire . . . oh! my father, save me, you should be here to kill me, the crab, where are you, my father, I have come here to find you, where did you go on that night of horror, when you stepped out into the fog? Are you sitting at the bottom of the sea or did you rise to the sun?

—   —   —   —

What good is it, to sit here and write, insanely. Do I hope thus to conjure the evil. The place is almost completely tumbled down. Twenty years of solitude, broken only twice. Twice we came here. But the mood did not last, the fine repentant mood. How different she was here, and even more beautiful, in this new garb of silent somberness. There was no tenderness, I was not the crab anymore—the last time especially.

How happy I was in the strength of my new-found manhood! How I cut wood, and hunted cunningly, and I ploughed a whole field. Why did we not stay? Was she not happier, then, even bathed in silent sorrow, a wild woman, telling me in the dark evenings by the fire, what she remembered, was she not happier than forgetting in the frenzy of lighted candelabra and panting desires under the rustle of silks. Ah! she is mad, she is a witch, she is evil, she belongs to the world of the monsters, she must be dragged down there, a jewel light for the orgy of those that dwell below.

— — — —

The weather has been beautiful the last few days, and instead of splitting pickets for a fence as I should have done, I went to the Cienaga, as a kind of pilgrimage. She took me there, once, that last time. I thought I would remember the spot where she told me that it was easy to lose the way. But when I started to go down on the other side of the Ridge* I was conquered immediately by the loneliness of the place. It was so silent except for the sudden screams of the blue jays. At times I could hear the pines on Longwood Ridge, rising on the other side of the steep canyon. It was like a rushing, buzzing thin noise and yet permeating everything. I was following the trail without paying much attention, and I must have passed that difficult spot where I should have turned, because I soon found myself in the bottom of the canyon in a place I did not remember at all. Then, instead of retracing my steps as would have been the wise way, I wrongheadedly tried to push on until I finally got to a place where it was impossible to even lead

---

*This is the ridge which rises at the mouth of the Sur and from there stretches to the south till the Hot Springs, surging out of the Ocean like a wall, so steep that the summit three thousand feet is only half a mile away from the edge of the water. This wall is of course folded into canyons that descend precipitously. There is a stream in each canyon and a little growth of redwoods, oaks, madrones, laurels, etc. The canyons are separated by rounded slopes covered with grass above the fogline and chaparral brush below. One gets the sensation that the whole thing ought to slide into the Ocean. Everything there, plants, animals or stones, leads a life of constant battle against gravity, hanging dizzily over the water. There are no flats anywhere to relieve the tenseness. The top of the ridge is a mere knife edge. On the other side it falls just as sharply, and from there on for a long way eastward, it is nothing but an inextricable labyrinth of canyons, ridges and spurs, an utterly wild country which serves to isolate the Coast from the interior valleys, lonely as even these are.

my horse, at least not without taking great risks. So I had to spend the night there and tie the beast to a tree for there was no feed anywhere. And so we spent a miserable night, he hungry, and I unable to sleep. I felt oppressed in the bottom of that ravine where I did not belong, with the myriad eyes of the night watching me. And I lost my way again twice, the next day. I fall into dreaming so often. But even if you watch it is easy to get lost in that place. The right way is often by turning off in another direction at perfectly non obvious places. You do not, you keep along an obvious path and suddenly find yourself in the midst of an impassable thicket.

But at last I arrived at the Cienaga, that mysterious bit of marsh in the heart of the hills, so startling with its reeds in the midst of these dry ravines and hillsides of brush. There is a hot spring nearby. I tried to find it, that evening, but did not succeed. The place held a great attraction for my father. He took my mother there several times. She forced him to do it. He did not want to take her along when he went there, for some reason, but she forced him thru that strange power of hers, that evil power, the power that is to be her undoing.

That time when she brought me here she was strangely agitated. We never slept that night. I kept throwing wood on the fire. She sat up the whole night, and watched intently the pond with her glaucuous eyes almost phosphorescent when the fire would die down. She never spoke at all. She spent the next day wandering around, looking for a certain waterfall nearby. But she could not find it. The next night she gave up watching the marsh. She lay down and she told me much of what had happened, and which she had never told me before. She spoke in stretches, between long silences. It was all very disconnected and at times I thought she must be asleep and speaking in her dreams, the things she said were so strange. It is only later by thinking and thinking that I have reconstructed the whole story, by piecing together the strange bits she dragged out of herself that night, with all the things she told me in the long evenings of that happy time when she and I lived here alone, and I thought it was going to be for ever. But we went back to that insane society life and she never spoke again of my father. Sometimes I doubt the whole tale, so unreal, so wild, so impossible. And how queer of her to have told these things to her son of fifteen. But then, has she ever treated me as a son? What am I but a slave, like any of her lovers, to be bullied, then cajoled, then played before, to be kicked again, and lashed with sarcasm and then kissed again passionately. The whore, the wench, the harlot, the witch! I must admire her clothes before she will wear them. I must approve the furniture for the new apartment. I must even approve the new lover. When I don't approve I am a vile thing, a misshapen creature, a hideous crab, so ugly that no woman will ever have me except for compassion. And then the tears and the repentance and the passionate kisses till I creep away in shame, from that divine body that makes men mad. Until I have broken away—but she will find me here. O my father, you poor madman, save me, rise out of the ocean, or come down from the sun, wherever you are, and keep her away from here. Keep the curse away, save your blood, kill me, kill the abomination surging rising into the lambent flame.

Oh! I am going mad! Why do I spend the hours recording my madness on the paper, instead of ploughing or chopping wood. The winter will soon be full on, and the bad weather, and no dry wood. But sometimes I think I will go utterly mad in this loneliness, if I don't speak to someone, even the paper. And sometimes I think perhaps I will feel better if I once puke the whole thing out. To write it, would not that be to conjure it, by giving a form to what lives a formless destructive life in my brain; and then, I will burn it.

— — — —

My father had been born here, but not my mother. On the contrary she was born in Paris, and she mixed in her blood all the races of Europe, it would seem, and even some in America, for she was in some way related to my father. The uncle who brought her up was very obscure about it. He was Russian, and had been a diplomat and still was a libertine in his old age. I imagine I remember him, a fantastic figure, half roué and half scholar, sometimes hopelessly drunk and sometimes very gentle and kind. Then he would take me on his knees and tell me strange tales of his adventures. He loved especially to tell those about the wild Indian tribes of Mexico, where his father held a post for many years. He was very fond of my mother whom he had adopted. It was he who told her of this place. For some obscure reason it was on his brain. He insisted that she must come here and find out what had happened to this branch of the family. At the same time he was most vague about it. He said he had gone there (meaning this place) once, years ago, and he had found two individuals living here, an Indian who spoke Spanish fluently and a young boy who spoke nothing but Indian altho he was apparently of white blood. The old Indian had been extremely wary and cautious for a long time, but finally when he became convinced that the man had not come to take away the boy, he acknowledged that the boy was a direct descendant of Don Bartolomeo de Merino, but absolutely refused to tell who were his father and mother. My uncle, or rather great uncle, then tried to find out thru the archives of the parish in Monterey. But these only mentioned two sons of Don Bartolomeo and his wife who died young. These two sons had also died young and unmarried. On the other hand, the old Indian swore solemnly that the boy was of unmixed white blood and the rightful heir of D.B. And there the enigma remained, to ferment at times in the mystic brain of my uncle. As he became older he increased both his libertinage and his piety, oscillating between moods of reckless license and brooding repentance. He died in one of these, speaking incoherently of retribution and atonement and urging my mother to undertake the voyage to California. He spoke of it as a pilgrimage. It became the idée fixe of his last days. Towards the end it became completely fantastic and he told my mother that it was her sacred duty to rescue her distant relative from a certain monster that held him prisoner in those wild mountains, even if she must sacrifice herself to the monster. She must do it in order to redeem our blood from the abominations.

All this must have had a very bad effect on my mother who was then a very young girl. She has told me, once, one of those evenings by the fire when she told me all these fantastic happenings, that she was utterly different then from what she became later on, after the "monsters from below took possession of my soul" as she expressed it. At the same time she acknowledges that she was far from being an innocent and blushing young maid. Her uncle had brought her up and educated her himself, and it would have been hard after that, to blush at anything. She knew too much—I merely repeat her words, for my own part I don't see how any one can know too much—and altho she had kept her own self away from vice it was not from revulsion or a sense of disgust, which she says she never felt (and I don't see how she could have developed it, having been from the first inured to it by the constant spectacle of her uncle's debaucheries—whom she knew on the other hand as a very good man and full of the inner value of things—very much the same thing has happened to myself). Well, as I was saying, she kept herself from vice not so much from a sense of decency as because it seemed to her futile. Her mind was possessed by the mysteries of ancient religions. Her uncle was a good scholar and had gathered an excellent library. She spent her life there, until she was eighteen, when he died.

Then she undertook the long trip to California, alone. She remembers it only as a nightmare. America was a great disillusion. She had imagined it as different, not these ugly wooden boxes sitting flatly on the ground, flaunting the indecent disorder of tin cans, wash lines, and helter-skelter machinery. The crowds of harsh, strident people seemed to have no connexion with the land. Their offensive familiarity made her recoil. Not even the immensities of the West could bring her out of that torpor where her froissé feelings had taken refuge. And so she landed in San Francisco still bewildered and hurt. She hurried down to Monterey, and started immediately for the Coast. She was aware in the old Spanish town of another atmosphere, quieter, more heedful of the demands of nature which must not be hacked and run over recklessly. She was aware of this, dimly, and of a land that was yet dreaming away—but she was still recoiled within her soul, immensely hurt by the clangor of the new culture thrown brutally in her face at this most perilous time of her life, so unprepared as she had been by the remote knowledge she had amassed in her uncle's library and the life, equally remote from the new reality, of a society which had preserved the old forms, mere dead skeletons that they were of true things that had been, while drowning its own death rattle in wit and merriment. She wanted to hurry on her mission, and go back.

In Monterey she could get very little information about the place she wanted to go. They spoke of it vaguely, as the "South Coast," the "Coast of the Sur." There was a stage that went there, or in that direction anyway, three times a week. No the stage did not go all the way down. It went as far as the road went, and from there on there was a trail, they said. No, there was no hotel at the end of the road, only a farm house. The people there would take her in for the night, surely. No they did not hire riding horses, but probably she could find someone around there who would lend her a horse and take her to where she wanted, if they knew where it was. Here no one knew of a Merino family, but perhaps they would be down there. Perhaps they would tell her down there and maybe they would not. They were a queer lot those who lived down the Coast, all mixed up in feuds, stealing each other's cattle, fighting. They very seldom came to Monterey, because it was too far. They got their provisions by boat from San Francisco—and much they raised themselves. There were very few people in those mountains, but they were a wild lot, suspicious, they did not want strangers in their country. There had been murders and dark things. These and other confidences, some of them utterly fantastic, she got from the stage driver, who himself confessed he had never gone beyond the end of the road. But she was not listening to him. She was now in an unreal state, almost a trance, the inevitable reaction to so many days of recoiling. She had left the world behind and she was traveling deeper and deeper into the unknown. The landscape was unreal, inhuman. The road skirted the shore where the sea heaved against huge black rocks and broke in insolent spurts of foam—and yet the ocean beyond was quite calm. For many hours they followed the sea, pressed against it by dreary hills—only twice did they pass a farm house, huddled low. In one place, a bearded man was waiting on horseback. He said "halloa," took a package of tobacco from the driver and rode off without another word. They went on and on. The driver now was silent. The road left the shore and entered the hills. It became a typical mountain road of the worst type, narrow, uneven, skirting the precipices. The four horses panted up the steep grades, dragging the rickety vehicle which creaked and sighed and appeared utterly exhausted. Finally they came to a slide in the mountainside. For several hundred feet an enormous slice of the hill had slid down into the canyon. Where the road had been there was now only an almost vertical wall of fresh loose earth. The driver stared at it silently for at least a minute. Then he said, "I guess we can't go no further. We will have to walk. There is a house on the other side of the hill." It was night when they finally got there. She was too tired to eat. She lay down on a pile of blankets the driver spread for her on the floor in a corner. For an interminable time, she heard the driver exchange gossip with their host, an old man with long white hair falling on his shoulders, keen blue eyes and a white mustache and pointed beard. He had only one tooth left and his speech was almost unintelligible, partly from the toothless condition of his mouth, partly from the fact that he spoke exceedingly fast and had a trick of repeating each statement four or five times in succession. ". . . and I said to him: keep a going, keep a going, never stop, never stop, that's the place where the Indian princess was buried, that's where she was buried, the well is awful deep, now, awful deep, awful deep, I got to have more rope, more rope, more rope. Keep agoing, I told him, keep agoing, never stop, never stop, I need just a little bit more rope . . ." The driver must have heard the story many times. He tried to drown the old man with his own words, in his low, tired, dragging voice, "I thought that damn place would slide again this winter. I told John last time I come thru, I says to him, 'that dirt ain't a going to hold, I says' . . ." And so the two voices went on for a long time, each one fighting for supremacy, until the old man won and the driver puffed silently at his pipe, staring somberly at the lamp. Finally they went to bed together in another corner of that disorderly shack. But even then the old man kept a continuous stream about princesses, gold, ropes, plots, vengeance and rights defrauded. He only stopped when he heard a loud snore from the driver. His feelings were hurt. He muttered "Damn you, sleep then, I won't tell you another thing." In an instant he was asleep himself, and snoring. She could not sleep. The two snores went on in different keys. Outside the horses were munching loudly. Once a coyote howled not very far, and the horses stopped munching for a moment and then resumed it again. She could not sleep, she felt oppressed, strange, unreal, uncomprehending. She was glad when the men got up even before dawn. They all ate breakfast in silence. The old man went out to hunt a horse in the pasture. The driver said to her, "He'll take you there. You can trust him. He is all right, a little bit off in the head, but harmless.

Well, goodbye, ma'am, I wish you luck. I don't like it much your going down that wild country all alone, but I guess if you got to go, you got to, t'ain't none of my business."

They started, she on a small gentle mare and the old man afoot. He walked ahead, with long strides, his white hair flying in the wind, swinging a staff with a martial air. He said he knew a short cut. They left the road and followed a trail. It was an abominably rough path. The old mare could hardly keep pace with the old man. Once the trail passed in front of a hut. A tall man very dirty and unkempt came to the door. He saw them pass by, sullenly, without a word. The old man carried his beard aggressively in the air and strode by, with an increase in the martial swing of the staff. After awhile he said, "he will be sorry some day, he will be sorry some day, keep a going, never stop, never stop, go somewhere, don't stop, no eat, no eat, no drink, no drink, ain't got time, keep a going, never stop," and then resumed his silent stride.

The country grew wilder and more mountainous. Her mind was now relaxing. Wild and remote the country was, frankly inimical to man, but it did not hurt her soul. It did not soothe her as a more amiable landscape would have done. She thought for a moment of the Touraine and laughed at the incongruity. Not even Switzerland of the grassy meadows. Perhaps Brittany came nearest, but yet so far. All these threw back at one something human, after all, some reflection of one's self, of one's ancestors. But here nothing was thrown back. The canyons grimaced inscrutably and the hillsides were in a dream. One felt like letting oneself go, be absorbed into the dream, sucked back into the disintegrated particles of earth baking on the hillsides. Perhaps then, one would live again and hear a multitude of voices speaking an archaic tongue.

She was jerked out of her dream. The Ocean lay under their feet, deeply blue, stretching away, away, indefinitely, to the West. And to the South an immense wall arose out of the water, seemingly endless. They had thus debouché upon the grand scene, at a bend of the trail. The Coast, the Coast of the Sur, there is no other spectacle on earth like it. I know what she felt, I have seen it. I have felt it, also. She was taken right out of this earth, at one stroke. It was another world, some world in a dream. And then she felt dizzy. They seemed to be flying, soaring far above the ocean. Down, down below some gulls were circling over the water. She let herself slide from the saddle. She closed her eyes and clung to the hillside, flattening her body against it. Dizzy, dizzy, dizzy. The sea was calling her. An immense fear swung her thru the spaces.

The old man came back to help her. "Come on, girlie, don't be afraid, t'ain't nothing, you'll get used to it, you'll get used to it. I got it the first time too. We got to go, we got to go, keep a going, never stop, never stop, no drink, no sleep, till you get there, keep a going, never stop, never stop." And he strode on martially, swinging his staff. She had to follow leading the mare. After awhile she found she could look down without getting so dizzy. Above the trail the hillsides rose in the same insane way. On some of them there were cattle and horses grazing peacefully, as if unaware of any danger. They crossed several canyons. The trail dipped into them. They plunged in forests of immensely tall redwoods, down into somber places where the ferns grew, then after crossing the stream, they reascended out of the woods once more into the sunlit immensity. Finally at one bend of the trail they came in sight of a canyon wider and deeper than the rest, and on the other side, perched way up, there was a cultivated field, a barn and several shacks. The whole looked so small and unreachable, like the nest of birds. The old man stopped. "There, that's where he lives, that's where he lives, he will be sorry some day. That's as far as I go, that's as far as I go. You'll have no trouble in finding the trail to his house, no trouble, no trouble, you'll find the trail to the left, after you cross the canyon, as soon as you get out of the brush, turn to the left and go up, go up, never stop, as soon as he sees you he'll shoot an arrow at you, you being a woman, and he hates women worse than men, that's why he shot the Indian princess, but he will be sorry, he will never get her gold, I'll get it as soon as I get a bit of rope, a bit of rope, the well is getting too deep, the old Indian was a bad one too, but he is dead now and the young one is worse yet, but he'll be sorry, he'll be sorry, well goodbye, ma'am."

She had no difficulty in finding the trail, as the old madman had said, but it took her a long time to climb. She had to rest many times.

The sun was half-way down, turning the ocean to gold. She passed under an immense cliff, then the trail became steeper yet, and at last she emerged onto a sort of plateau where the ground was less steep. Three deer bounded away at the sight of her. She passed by several fields bound by tumbled down picket fences. The place had been evidently cultivated with care at one time, but now it was fast reverting to the wilds. She passed a barn and corrals. A horse stood tied to a post, saddle still on. From there a sort of lane led to a group of shacks ranged in a semi-circle. In the open space at the center a man was bending over a short post stuck in the ground, working a deerhide. He was naked to the waist and wore the buckskin moccasins and leggins of Indians, and another loin cloth of buckskin twisted from his belt, leaving the thighs bare. He was working hard, stretching the hide from end to end over the edge of the post, and his brown skin glistened in the sun. But his long hair tumbled forward was of a brown red, and when he straightened up at her approach, she saw that his eyes were blue. He looked at her for a moment, then he said in broken Spanish, "I know you come. Several days I feel a noise in my ear like rush of air and I know very well no use fighting." And he resumed the stretching work on the deer hide. She stood there, feeling very uncomfortable. She was thinking about something very strange in his face, some unconnectedness, a mixture of something kind and another thing unfriendly, something that was real and something else uncanny. But she was too tired to think, and since he paid no further attention to her she walked into the house.

She was tired, dizzy, disoriented. She wanted to rest, to shut out the immensity of space. She sat on a block of wood by the fire. She closed her eyes and let time go by, vaguely conscious that the day was getting dark.

She was startled out of her doze by his entrance. He had a few chunks of venison skewered on a stick which he placed before the fire to roast. He also warmed a pot of beans and gave her some in a calabash, along with a couple of maize cakes. All this in silence. She hardly dared look at him. There was something feral and disquieting in all his movements, lithe, steely, always poised. They sat by the embers in the dark for a long time. She felt, uncomfortably, that he was looking at her. Once more she was aware of that puzzling double something in his face. She could endure the silence no longer. She said, "Do you want to know who I am and why I came?" "I know already." His answer puzzled her. How could he possibly know? But was any of this possible? How had she come here? and for what purpose? did she know it herself? did she even know who she really was? did he not perhaps know all these things better than she did? She was lost in a strange land where he was at home. She was in his power. She felt a wave of alarm, then of defense, then of aggressive hatred rising in her against this silent, inexplicable, half-human being. All of her womanly grace and charm rose tumultuously in her, outraged, defying his moroseness.

He rose and threw some fagots on the fire. He took a brand and went out. She heard him go into another house. He reappeared with a pile of deerskins and two heavy bearskins. He made her a bed of these on the earthen floor. A similar bed was rolled up against the wall. He stretched himself on this, but lay for a long time, leaning on his elbow, watching the fire, before lying down with his head on a block of wood. She lay motionless, alert, sleepless for a long time. She heard his breath in and out regularly. He was a restless sleeper, threshing about, muttering in his dreams. The shack was far from dark. The moon was half full and through the wide open window she watched the tall redwood over the barn. Once she rose to get a drink. She threw a few twigs on the fire to make a light. While she was drinking slowly from the calabash, enjoying the cold mountain water, she watched him. He was lying on his side, the billet of wood pushed out of the way, the face resting on the extended arm. It was very gentle, even wistful. The flame died down. She threw some more twigs. They flared up. He turned his face away, suddenly, on the other side. She almost shrieked. It was not the same face. This was full of a malign evil, cold, cruel. He stirred uneasily, and drew a skin over his shoulders and head. She crept back to her bed, and watched again the open window. She was getting drowsy. She also felt at times the dizziness of the trail and she shook the invading torpor. The window was there, the fire still flickered, the walls were very dimly lit. All that was firm and solid. It was not sliding down into the Ocean. She was getting drowsy again. She watched the window. It was white in the moonlight. White like alabaster. The alabaster of corpses. She was a dead Indian princess. She had been buried in a cave in the middle of a desert. That was thousands of years ago. She lay, waiting, waiting, waiting for someone. He was coming. He was nearing. She heard him approach like a rush of wind. He leapt on the window-sill. Oh my God! he was a tiger . . . She shrieked in terror. She lay trembling, bathed in sweat. She heard his voice asking sleepily: "What's matter. Bad dream?" "Who was he?" she asked. "Who who?" "Someone was here just now." "No, nobody. You just bad dream, go to sleep." She was gathering her wits. What an absurd question. Of course nobody had been here. And yet . . . yes, there had been a presence here, she was sure of it, she could feel it still, lingering, not far. My God! what was that? That scream, outside, that demoniac yell . . . and there again, what she-devil in her agony . . . once more, far off, diminishing in the distance . . . she lay trembling . . . she heard him mutter "mountain lion" and grumble something else in a strange tongue. That's what it was, then. She remembered having read somewhere about the terrifying scream of the puma, almost like the voice of a woman in terror. She tried to sleep again. But she could not still her fear. She was now utterly scared. She would have liked to creep under his covers, take refuge with him. No he was too non-human, too eerie for comfort. Only more fear would come out of him like a leaping sword. And then, suddenly, the meaning of her pilgrimage became clear to her, and now she quivered under her covers, with shame, with terror, with desire, during the long hours of the night. She heard him breathing quietly. She wondered which side of his face was up. She was afraid.

When she woke at dawn he was already gone. She went to sleep again and slept for a long time. The sun was high in the sky when she woke again. She went out. She felt exhilarated. She drank avidly the splendid beauty of the place. She was not dizzy any longer. Surely there could not be any evil spirits around here. It was too beautiful, too calm. She wandered around. She followed a path under oak trees. A flock of wild pigeons flew off with a great noise of flapping wings. They circled and lit on top of a redwood up the hill. Then a covey of quail ran across a clearing, whistling with apprehension. She came to the edge of the next canyon. And once more she felt dizzy looking down on a sea of tree tops. How many wild things were at this moment creeping silently along secret trails? She walked back to the house. She wondered where he was. She went around the corrals, through the stables. His horse was not there. The place became silent and lonely. She was hungry. She ate. Then she wondered how those cakes of maize were made. She wondered what she could do to help him. Was it possible in any way to help him? She swept the earthen floor with a short broom made of sage. It smelt nice. All the rooms were very orderly, but she tried to put still more order. She took down a pair of buckskin breeches from a rafter. They were torn. She wondered how these things were mended, with what kind of thread. She felt so helpless in such strange surroundings, so lonely. How could he live in such utter loneliness. She imagined how he must have missed the old Indian who had raised him. She went out again towards the barn. There was there an open space. It was directly over that high perpendicular cliff she had passed under on her way up the day before. She looked down a thousand feet of sheer cliff. She recoiled with dizziness. But she wanted to conquer her fear and she came back again and sat on a large stone mortar that stood there, just near the edge. It is there yet. It is one of those mortars the Indians used to mash acorns in, chestnuts and other foods. But I have never seen one as large as this: it is almost knee high. I like to sit on it and watch the Ocean. There seems to be some mysterious force in it, that penetrates your own body. I have been very sad and restless these last few days. Sometimes I feel that I can't stand the suspense any longer, that I must run away to somewhere where she will not find me. But when I sit on that stone I forget everything. I just sit and look at the edge of the world, over the sea. I seem to become a stone myself, just a part of the earth, a tree perhaps or an animal warming himself in the sun. And at the same time I feel something bad in that mortar, some evil, something too strong for us to control. It is somehow connected with misfortunes in our family. I think mother knows something which she will not tell me. I don't know. I can't tell since coming here, I feel all sorts of dark things I never experienced before. I know my mother felt the same thing about that mortar, I mean that same quieting power, that sucking of your own self back into a stone of the soil. She often went and sat on it.

She felt it that very first time, waiting there, wondering where he had gone, feeling lonely.

When he came the sun was already quite low, almost in the ocean. First she heard a confused noise of branches cracking, the neighing of horses and the booming sound of their footfalls. They emerged from the woods up on the hillside, about a hundred feet higher than the barn, and they ran down the pasture, biting and kicking, mane and tail in the wind, bucking and sliding, each one eager to arrive first at the water trough for a place of vantage. I love to watch the horses coming down to water. It's a grand sight. If I hear them in time I always run out to watch them. Especially in the late afternoon when the sun shines on their glossy coats. Here they come, running down the slope, kicking, bucking, sliding, in a waterfall of fire. Yi-ah . . . wu-yi . . . yi-ah-wu . . . yi . . . yi! And behind the caballada he came; holding his own excited horse, himself so quiet, so full of that springlike poise that never left him. He rode bareback—his own horse he had turned loose in the bunch and he had jumped on a tall sorrel of whom he was especially fond—he rode with his body thrown back, his toes dug in the arm pits of his horse, legs and thighs like an arc of steel, and the torso rippling on the hips with every plunge of his horse. He looked like some kind of god-animal, she said.

He seemed happy, in his own silent way, even playful. He sneaked up to a foal who had buried his nose in his mother's breasts, and caught him by an ear and a forefoot. The foal reared and tried frantically to free himself, dragging his captor around the corrals. The man was laughing, nimbly avoiding the small kicking hoofs. After fury and indignation had subsided, trembling still with fear, the foal submitted to being stroked. Twice he tried to escape and each time he found himself suddenly lying flat on his panting side, in the dust of the corral. Finally he was permitted to rejoin his mother and soothe his ruffled feelings with warm milk.

They went to the house. They ate in silence. She began to understand that communication with him was not thru words. She felt less fear of him, less strangeness. She managed to sit on the good side of his face and now she could look at him. She even stared after she discovered that he did not even notice it. She wondered how it would

116

feel to be loved by him. She was vexed when he said, "You sleep other house. Too much bad dream." Except when her uncle was in rage, it was she who had ruled his household. She had always kept his mistresses from establishing themselves in the house. Revel in it, even carry the debauche to the point of saturnalia, they might, she herself presided in her cool, absentminded fashion, untouchable behind her green eyes. She had learned to repulse many an attack. She was therefore quite unprepared to see herself thus unceremoniously sent to bed. She gasped. She rose in offended dignity. She summoned all the weapons of sex. She stalked out of the house, looking more lovely, more desirable than the goddess of lust. He came after her, carrying her bundle of pelts. He looked puzzled. He said, "What's matter, you mad?" She collapsed on the pelts, she buried her face in the fur to stifle her laughter. She could not. She laughed convulsively, hysterically. She was shaken with sobs. She cried and laughed for a long time, until she slept.

Vaguely, in her sleep, she heard the mountain lions shriek that night. She was not disturbed. If they come in here I will laugh in their face, she thought sleepily. She slept soundly.

In the morning he caught two of the horses and harnessed them to the plough, an antiquated affair, practically home-made. The share was all that remained of the original plough brought over the trail years ago, on top of a mule. A young sapling of laurel, carefully chosen in the forest for its curve, served as a handle. Pressing on the end of it, or lifting it by bodily strength, was the only means of regulating the depth of the furrow. It probably would have been impossible to manage it in any other than this loose loam on this steep field. But here the share opened the earth and it fell over like a stream, and the patch of velvety dark brown earth grew larger and larger. Sometimes the share plunged its nose too deep in the soil, and the horses stopped and fretted, while he bore on the end of the beam and moved it from side to side to disengage it. He was entirely naked save for his loincloth. It was hard work. The horses were wet. His face was grimy with the dust. His eyes were wide with excitement, and when all three stopped at the end of a furrow his chest heaved in deep breaths.

She had watched the stolid peasants follow the slow moving ploughs, at home. They dragged enormous shoes, tramping on the fresh clods. When she came near, an acrid stench escaped from under their sweat imbibed heavy shirts and underwear. They followed the plough slowly, at the same pace always, their eyes vague and somnolent. She laughed at the contrast. She wondered if they felt, even in the lowest layer of their somnolent souls, that they were raping their mother.

He ploughed all that week. She had gradually assumed all the housework. She had begun to scrape a deer hide. It made her back ache. She enjoyed it. Sometimes now he spoke in the evening. She did not always understand what he said, but she felt he was less lonely. He spoke of things the horses had said. He seemed to be in communication with a world, new to her, but not strange, curiously enough—something she had known in her childhood, and forgotten. She felt the same thing when she rode with him, sometimes, to help him round up cattle or horses. They would sit down, at some spring, under oaks and madrones. They loosened the saddle cinchas. The horses drank long draughts, and then rested on one foot, hanging their heads. They themselves sprawled on the light and shadow mottled ground, and he would speak of the things. She had heard clever men speak of the soul of nature, she had read poetical sentiments in verse. It had always sounded flat and dead to her. Now she knew why, or rather she felt it without knowing precisely wherein lay the reason. Also she remembered old nursery tales and vaguely, very vaguely scraps of forgotten childish emotions. And sometimes, also, scraps of mythological tales emerged in her mind, incongruously, out of classical dusty volumes. She tried to understand whether he was speaking of the trees or of people in the trees. Certain rocks were to him like supernatural beings, and others were just rocks, and sometimes the difference seemed to lie in the surrounding circumstances. She was puzzled. She felt his strangeness. At other times, she gave up trying to analyze. She abandoned herself to a growing feeling that seemed to arise out of the blades of grass, the bits of stones, the bark of the trees and the green colour of the leaves sharp against the blue sky. Then she understood him, no, felt him better. It was all the same thing and he was part of it, let it all conquer her. She submitted herself. It was all one thing and made up of separate parts. And the parts were like air, like breaths, they floated about, they became the whole suddenly. Perhaps that's what he was talking about.

He said very simple things, unconnected, like a child—only it meant something. She had heard men and women argue brilliantly, scholars like her uncle, and so often she had felt it meant nothing.

He told her a little; very guardedly, about some beings who must be respected and propitiated. Sometimes he called them the "owners of the springs," or the "masters of the hunt," and again and again "the keepers of those that fly above" which appeared to include the clouds as well as the birds and also the words of speech. All these had to be propitiated and spoken to by their names. But their names he would not reveal to her, because she was a woman. At first this angered her, but she came to realize that this was no assumption of superiority on his part. On the contrary he seemed to vaguely feel that she herself, as woman, was one of those beings. She was a keeper of something. It would be dangerous for what she kept if she were given the knowledge of these things. "You must know them in a different way, your own way," he told her once. "Maybe they will tell you their names, maybe in a dream, maybe just your heart will tell you. That's your name, not mine and you must never tell me." But she was not satisfied with that. She wanted to know his. She felt she would not possess him, until she did. She asked. Then he grew silent and morose. They would mount their horses again and look for the cattle in the deep gullies, on the edges of copses. She was learning to ride well. She was no longer dizzy. She even enjoyed riding on the steep hillsides, galloping straight down into the void over the rolling edge of a pasture, with the ocean shimmering so far below. Hot after the wild cattle, to keep them from sliding into the refuges of wooded canyons. She learned to be alert and quick, to read the minds of animals. She wanted to please him, and he was a hard master, altho he never scolded or even criticized her. But when she did well he was immensely pleased and became gentle and almost a comrade.

She wanted him. She knew it, now, definitely. And she knew she was yet far from possessing him. Did he want her and was he keeping himself away for some reason? She could not tell. She knew she was desirable. Even if she had not been told so by many a roué, she would have known it of her own knowledge. But was she desirable to him? It was impossible to tell. Sometimes she thought, and with despite, that if she could become a mere stone, or an animal or a cloud, then he would see her charms. But how could she do that? How could she penetrate that strange world of his spirits, so near and so remote? She hated them, she felt they stood in the way, she wanted to destroy them, blindly.

He seemed to read her thoughts. He became sombre and distant. Once or twice she caught a strange look on his face, a beseeching look, humble, a prayer. She was stirred, deeply. What did he want her to do? Wasn't it something too difficult for her, something she could not do, she did not know how to do?

She still slept in that hut, away from him. Sometimes she heard at night, that unearthly cry of the puma. It always drove her to madness. She was no longer afraid of it. She hated it. Sometimes she would be awake for hours, waiting for it. There it came, way off, at first, then nearer and nearer, fiendish. Once or twice she ran out in the night, recklessly. She felt she would have the strength to strangle the demon or puma or whatever it was. She found only the empty mysterious night.

When the ploughing was done, he asked her to sow the grain. He asked her diffidently, bashfully. She was surprised and delighted. Then she realized that in some obscure way she was performing a ceremony full of emotion for him. At first she was awkward, but gradually she acquired freedom of motion and she spread the seed with a fine gesture. A strange intoxication mounted in her. She felt his eyes on her. She felt closer to him than she ever had, before. He seemed very happy. He said, "That seed will grow well. You must keep thinking about it in your heart. Think good thoughts in your belly. It will grow well."

But when she was alone, she became full of despair. She did not know how to think in her belly. She felt him more remote than ever. A black rage mounted in her. She wanted him. She would have him, even if she must kill all his spirits. Then she thought, "I can't think good thoughts in my heart, but I think bad ones. Ah! the seed will not grow, now." She cried in her misery and she waited for that cursed yell outside in the night.

Why could she not think in her heart? If only she had, it would have been all different. Instead of a crab I would be beautiful like my father. We would have been happy. I would not have had to fight with that unnameable horror. She would not have become a witch. She was not a witch, then, at that time. What was it that she must do, then? I don't know myself, it's all dark. But she cursed his spirits and became a witch, to have him. And she gave birth to a crab. O my mother, stay away from me, do not come, do not come, don't you see the unnameable horror?

The rainy season was full on. I am writing this in the same house where they spent so much of their time when the weather drove them indoors for days at a time. They sat by the fire and worked on hides. They made garments. He told her many stories, that winter, long stories of the time when there were other men walking about the earth, men animals. But she was not listening with her heart. Her heart had become black. She sat looking at him, desiring him, desiring his destruction.

The winter is full on, now. I have not cut enough fire wood. I have to go out constantly and cut more. It is wet and cold and nasty outside. The rain comes in a drizzle, whipped by the south wind. You can't see the ocean. At times only, thru a rent in the fog. It is angry and white with foam. I feel restless and nervous. I went out this afternoon. I walked in the fog and the rain, raging at the storm. I wanted to howl. Tonight I am full of black thoughts.

But there are beautiful days, here, even in the winter time, days when the sun comes out to warm the grass growing on the hillsides. Good days for hunting. Even at noon it is not too hot and the deer do not lie in the brush as in summer. He did all the hunting, and never allowed her to come. He did not even let her touch his gun, an old muzzle loading rifle. He also used a bow and arrows, to spare the ammunition. And these also she must not touch.

Every month, at the new moon, he disappeared for two or three days. "I am going to the Cienaga. I will come back after while." "Are you looking for cattle?" "Yes, cattle and things." But she knew that it was some mysterious affair. She wanted to go with him. But he would not take her. Then she begged him to take her, or to stay because she was afraid alone. She was afraid of the puma, screeching around the house.

He was very much perplexed. He had become very fond of her. "I must go," he said. "I must go. It must be done. You must not come.

It is not good for you." She promised she would not ask anything, she would not look at anything, but she did not want to be left alone.

Finally he consented and they went there. It was in the springtime. She had only been on the other side of the ridge a few times, and alone, never with him. And now she was sorry she had come. Not only the wild, remote, uncanny country gave her an uneasy, almost terrifying feeling, but the change in his countenance was even more terrible. Something utterly savage had crept into him. He rode paying no heed to her. Once in a while he uttered a strident yell. It made her shiver every time. She urged her horse to keep pace. Sometimes the trail was dangerous. He rode on, not heeding her. The look on his face became more savage, exalted, inhuman.

They arrived at the Cienaga at dusk. They unsaddled their horses. They hobbled their horses and turned them loose. They made camp. She ate but he did not touch the food. She lay down on one side of the fire. He lay down on the other side. She could not sleep, she was stiff with fear. She dreamed awake, shreds of dreams, fantastical. Once she saw him rise. He crept over to her side. She was petrified with fear. He bent over her. She could not stand the look on his face. She closed her eyes for an instant. When she opened them again, he was lying on his side of the fire. She wondered if she had dreamed. She could not tell between dream and reality.

In the morning he went away. He told her he would be gone all day. She must not follow him. She must not leave this spot. If she did he would surely kill her. He walked off with his bow and arrows.

After he went, she felt less terrified. Her mind was numb. She began to doze. The day dragged by interminably. The hobbled horses were grazing not far. She dozed. She heard a muffled sound, in the distance, a rhythmic booming sound. She half dreamed that it was her own heart buried deep in the ground.

He came back late in the afternoon. He looked tired and wearied. There were traces of paint on his face and on his chest and arms. The wall of granite on the other side of the marsh was red in the evening glow. The marsh was already in gloaming. He waited until it was quite dark, then he ate. He let the fire die quite low, only glowing embers. He did not lie down. He squatted, watching the wall of granite, rising in a dark mass against the indigo sky. At last the crescent moon appeared, so young and thin. Now he threw more wood on the fire and he lay down to sleep.

— — — —

The spring was coming to an end, too soon. The hillsides showed a subtle yellow in the green. In some places the grass was already heading, and not yet knee high. And the crop of grain looked thin and wan. He was worried and somber. When they rode together he did not speak to her anymore. He avoided the springs.

But she grew restless and she rode alone, now, often. She did not feel fear any longer, but rather a sort of exaltation, some dark spirit of power and strength which drove her from the house to wander in the fields, singing wild melodies she did not understand. And once she even stole his bow and arrows and shot an eagle. She did not dare bring it home, but hid the feathers in a canyon in a hollow tree. And now she often went there and stuck the feathers in her hair and danced madly, by herself.

Ah, now she understood the wild country. She understood its secret. She gloried in that feeling of strength and power. She was drunk with it.

She began even to think of hunting that puma. She hated her. She hated her violently. She knew it was a female. She must destroy it. She would wait in the dark and watch her and some day she would take the arrows again and kill her.

And one day, after she had danced madly in the canyon, she hid a feather in her breast and she came home. That night she concealed herself behind the barn and she waited. At last she heard it, the fiendish yell, way off, in the distance, then nearer and nearer. She waited, all her senses on the alert, peering intently. There it came, the long, tawny shape, past her, slow, out into the moonlight that flooded the path to the houses, stalking, nonchalantly, insolently, but silent. She saw her jump in at the open window of his shack, stand poised for an instant on the sill, and then disappear within.

And now her rage made her bold and reckless. She followed. She also stepped insolently and noiselessly. She held the gun. She went to the shadow side of the house. She knew where there was a knot hole.

She looked in. The light of the fire was flickering. He always kept the fire burning all night even in the warmest nights. He was lying with his head on his arm, the evil side up, sleeping restlessly as usual. The beast was walking to and fro, from one end of the shack to the other. She was purring very low, like the rumble of distant thunder. Then she lay down by the side of the man, head resting on extended paws, the tip of the tail only moving, waving from side to side. He still slept, restlessly.

She could not introduce the muzzle and aim at the same time. A violent hatred shook her body. She fumbled the eagle feather. She crept around the house inch by inch, noiselessly, until she was under the open window. She looked in. He was sleeping restlessly. In the distance, she heard a wild scream, and further away, diminishing in the distance.

The summer was coming in, fast. The hillsides now were turning quite yellow. Hardly the faintest green left. And now the crop, too, in spite of the careful ploughing, was turning yellow. He went around dejected. He sat for hours and hours in the sun, on that mortar, blinking in the sun, hopelessly.

One day he said to her, "I think you must help. It's all wrong but I don't understand any more, and the old man is gone. I am blind, now, and deaf. I have asked the springs, I have asked the birds. I have asked all the keepers of the world, but they don't speak to me. Even my own protector has gone. I am all alone now, blind and deaf and useless. You try it. Maybe you can, maybe it's for you, maybe you have the power. I know what you have been doing. I found the feathers in the canyon. I can't stop you now. My power is all gone. Now you try to save us."

She was deeply moved and alarmed. She felt pity now for this man whom she had feared so much. And still she must turn to him with a question, "What can I do? How is it to be done?" He showed the least anger. "Haven't you found out? What have you been doing then, playing around the springs, opening the secret places?" She retorted in anger, "You are a fool, I know more than you think. I will make it rain." And she went off in bravado. She danced madly in the canyons, she shot many birds, all kinds, and strew their feathers around, she danced and sang. At times she grew mad and ate grass and leaves. Some of them were poisonous and made her sick and more crazy yet. He sat, listlessly, blinking in the sun. At last he roused himself, one evening. "You can't do it, that way. You don't know how. That way you will only do harm. That's a witch's way. The keepers of the world are only annoyed by your foolishness. I think you have power now. But you don't know how to use it. Maybe I must teach you. I think it is all wrong. I don't know any more. I am blind. I have lost all my power. I'll tell you and then you try. We will go to the Cienaga to-morrow. There is a great power there. Maybe you can use it and save us. You will have to be careful."

She could hardly sleep that night. She was elated, excited. She felt confident in herself. She was full of power. She could save them if he only told her some of these things he had hoarded so foolishly, so selfishly for himself.

They started early. She rode in the van. And she yelled as he had yelled, bravely, defiantly. He followed, thinking, preoccupied, worried. He told her not to yell. "We are not doing that kind of thing, now. We don't want them to hear us. We are doing something dangerous, now."

They arrived. They unsaddled their horses. They hobbled their horses and turned them loose. They made camp. He told her not to eat, but she was hungry and ate. They sat by the fire and he began to tell her things.

"I can't make rain. It doesn't belong to me. My protector is not of the rain people. "Who is your protector?" she asked, insolently. "I won't tell you that. You don't need to know that." She laughed. "You don't need to tell me. I know who she is. I know some things too." He looked alarmed. She liked to torture him. She continued, "She is beautiful, your protector, and she has such a sweet, powerful voice. She sings so beautifully at night." He looked crushed. He was trembling. He mumbled. "You know too much. It's you who have taken my power." They sat a long time in silence, she exultant, he dejected. He resumed. "Well, alright, you know too much. And you don't know enough. Maybe it's for you to make rain. Maybe you belong to the water people. I don't know who your protector is. I don't ask you. The old man told me women have no protectors. Perhaps he was wrong. He said himself that he did not know all of it. Maybe you have a protector. I don't know what your name is. I have never asked you." All her vanity was aroused. She thought furiously. She felt full of power. She made her heart answer. She spoke defiantly. "I must not reveal my name to you. But I have a protector. He lives in a dark place, and when he comes out in the sun his back shines like the shells from the sea . . ." "Yes, yes, hush, don't call him now. Yes, you know. Yes, yes, he is powerful. I am afraid of him. He lives there in the waterfall. He is more powerful than my protector. I am afraid of him. That's why I yell when I come here, to scare him. He must not come while I speak to the moon. He would eat her. All right, you go to the waterfall to-morrow. You will find my drum there under the rock. You make the rain, then. All this is bad. I don't like it. I am afraid."

She was excited. She could not sleep. When morning came, he told her how to find the waterfall. He would not go with her. She took his arrows. She went the way he had said. She slid down that smooth wall of rocks from ledge to ledge, without fear. It was dark in the bottom of the canyon. The light filtered green through the elms and sycamores. She followed the stream, up, as he had said. She came to the waterfall. It falls into a deep pool. It is a weird place, there. The other day when I went there I saw a large trout come to the surface and go down again. Or at least I thought I did. Maybe I imagined it only. The place is just a narrow slit in the hills, the canyon is very deep and narrow there, and the fall makes a deafening noise.

I don't know what my mother did there, that day. She would not tell me. She only said she found the drum and took off her clothes, and sang and danced all day, and then something happened at sunset. Something terrible she said. She would not tell me what. But she said it frightened her and at the same time drove her mad, quite insane.

She threw the drum into the pool, and grabbed the arrows and the bow and fled. She was utterly scared. She must haved passed the cliff without seeing it. She climbed out of the canyon at the wrong place and became lost in the woods. It was quite dark now. She was running, falling, stumbling, crying into fear. Then she heard the wild scream of her enemy and she stood frozen. She heard it again, nearer, and again nearer, now almost plaintive, querulous. She crouched in the shadow of a tree. The hatred was now stronger than the fear. She took an arrow out of the quiver. She strung it. The tawny thing appeared and stopped uneasily, growling low. She took careful aim behind the shoulder. The string hummed. The beast crumpled and beat the air convulsively with her paws for a moment, then lay still. Now she ran again, once more drowned in anguish and fear. Now she saw the light of the camp fire through the trees. She ran again. If she could only reach it before that other dreadful thing, lurking about, found her. She stopped. She could not see the fire any more. It was pitch dark. There must be something standing between her and the fire. There was a presence. There was someone there in front of her. She felt the iciness of terror creep through her. She put out her hand. Horror! She felt a human body. Avid hands crept under her arm pits. She felt a dizzy, smothering, sickening dissolution of her entrails. Her body was being rent. She surrendered to the monster. She wanted it.

The sun was already shining when she came to her senses. She was lying by the camp fire. She felt terribly exhausted, dazed, yet. She saw him come with the horses. He saddled them. He looked very tired and very sad. He also looked very beautiful and human for the first time. But a shadow was over him.

They traveled thru the labyrinth of canyons, slowly. He stopped often to ask her how she felt, if she was tired. She was still dazed. She tried to ride her horse next to his whenever the trail was wide enough. She wanted passionately to be out of the wild country. She did not want to be left behind in the place of dark powers.

They came at last to the great ridge. The sky was cloudy, but there was no wind. It was hot and sultry. The sea was dark, glassy. It looked sinister. They rested. They unloosed their saddle cinches. They sat on a rock. He was silent. She tried to cheer him up. "See, it is going to rain." He looked at the somber sky. "Yes, it is going to rain. Your crop will grow," and he tried to smile, but he shuddered. He was silent for a long time. Then he spoke again. "The old man would never tell me who my father and mother were. He said I must never know. But he swore to me that I was the direct descendant of Don Bartolomeo de Merino. Your child will be the rightful owner. I knew you would come. Now it is all dark."

They cinched their horses and descended to the ranch. Large drops of rain were already falling. Suddenly a strong wind arose, whirling, and died down again. They went inside and lit a fire. The wind rose again, whipping fogs over the water. The surface of the ocean was now seething, white with foam. The rain came in torrents, beating on the roof with a deadening noise. The wind increased. It became a terrific storm with the darkness. It howled and shrieked, shaking the house, rattling the windows. They heard the crash of a falling tree, not far, in the woods. A bird came headlong against the window pane, startling them. They crouched near the fire. Suddenly she heard, far away, the dismal shriek of a puma. He rose like a ghost, walked to the door and went out. She rushed after him, but the wind was pushing so strongly against the door that she could not open it. In a madness of despair she threw herself against it and finally pushed it far enough to slip out. The wind and the torrents of rain blinded her, strangled her, threw her about. She gripped the picket fence. She called and called in the night. She dragged herself step by step along the fence. She reached the barn. She called and called. She dragged herself on her knees. She knocked herself against something hard. It was the stone mortar. She shrieked with horror and embraced it convulsively, dizzy with terror, all that night, while all the demons of darkness raged around her.

It must have been terrible after that, for her, all alone, in that place. Yet she said she did not mind it so much. She did not even miss him. Sometimes he seemed so remote, so unreal, that she remembered him only as a dream. Besides her mind was blank, dull. She just lived like an animal, carrying my life inside, heavier and heavier, in a dream. But after I was born, she awoke again, and then she could not endure it any longer. And she went back to the world. Why didn't we stay? We would have been happy.

I would be happy, now, I would forget everything, if I didn't fear her coming. The storm is almost at an end, and the sun will soon come out and the trail will be open again. Oh my father, keep her away, come back with the sun and take her away, save me from the abomination.

I went to the Cienaga. I went to the waterfall. She was there. My father, why did you not come and save me!

My mind is splitting asunder. Who am I? He is on a journey, the long journey through the dark places, the endless space where time roars. Who is he? I am the Crab, the monster from below.

'

Bibliography of Jaime de Angulo
by Wendy Leeds-Hurwitz

1911 The 'Trial' of Ferrer. New York: New York Labor News Co.

1922-3 Los Sonidos Nasales en las Lenguas Indigenas de Mexico. Ethnos series 2, 1(1)55-58.

1924 On the Religious Feeling Among the Indians of California. The Laughing Horse 10:[22-25, 27-30].

1925a Kinship Terms in Some Languages of Southern Mexico. American Anthropologist 27(1):103-107.

1925b Five Thousand Years. The Independent 115(3918):11-12.

1925c Taos Kinship Terminology. American Anthropologist 27(3): 482-483.

1925d Do Indians Think? The Laughing Horse 12:9-12.

1925e Don Bartolomeo. The Independent 115(3923):149-151, 167; 115(3924):179-180, 195-196, 115(3925):215-216, 223; 115 (3926):243-245, 251-252.

1925f The Linguistic Tangle of Oaxaca. Language 1(3):96-102.

1926a Two Parallel Modes of Conjugation in the Pit River Language. American Anthropologist 28(1):273-274.

1926b Review of La Covada y el Origin del Totemismo by Enrique Casas. American Anthropologist 28(1):286.

1926c The Background of Religious Feeling in a Primitive Tribe. American Anthropologist 28(2):352-360.

1926d Review of The Basque Dialect of Marquina by William Rollo. American Anthropologist 28(2):437-438.

1926e   The Development of Affixes in a Group of Monosyllabic Languages of Oaxaca. Language 2(1):46-61; 2(2):119-133.

1926f   The Wife of Cheating Frog. The Independent 117(3977):206-207.

1926g   L'Emploi de la Notion d' "etre" dans la Langue Mixe. Journal de la Societe des Americanistes de Paris n.s. 18:1-7.

1926h   Tone Patterns and Verb Forms in a Dialect of Zapotek. Language 2(4):238-250.

1926i   Review of La Festin d'Immortalite, Etude de Mythologie Comparee Indoeuropeenne and Le Crime des Lemniennes, Rites et Legendes du Monde Egeen by Georges Dumezil. American Anthropologist 28(3):560-562.

1927a   Religious Emotion vs. Social Emotion. American Anthropologist 29(1):150-152.

1927b   Review of Pratiques des Harems Marocains by A.-R. de Lens. American Anthropologist 29(1):124.

1927c   Review of L'art et la Philosophie des Indiens de l'Amerique du Nord by Hartley Burr Alexander. American Anthropologist 29(3):351-354.

1927d   Texte en Langue Pomo (Californie). Journal de la Societe des Americanistes de Paris n.s. 19:129-144.

1928a   The Sun. The Laughing Horse 15:[28-29].

1928b   Review of Myth in Primitive Psychology by Bronislaw Malinowski. American Anthropologist 30(2):322-326.

1928c   Tribute to Robinson Jeffers. The Carmelite, Robinson Jeffers Supplement, p. 4.

1928d   La Psychologie Religieuse des Achumawi. Anthropos 23:143-166, 561-589.

1929a   Metodologia Linguistica. Quetzalcoatl 1(1):11-14; 1(2):19-22.

1929b   A Tfalati Dance-Song in Parts. American Anthropologist 31(3):496-498.

1929c   Grammatical Processes: Incremental vs. Autonomic. Language 5(2):117-118.

1930a   A Practical Scheme for a Semantic Classification. Anthropos 25:137-146.

1930b   Review of An-nik-a-del. The History of the Universe as told by the Mo-des-se Indians of California recorded and edited by C. Hart Merriam. American Anthropologist 32(1):172-175.

1931a   The Lutuami Language (Klamath-Modoc). Journal de la Societe des Americanistes de Paris n.s. 23:1-45.

1931b   The Man Who Went to the Land of the Dead: A California Indian Tradition. The Laughing Horse 19:1-7.

1932   The Chichimeco Language (Central Mexico). International Journal of American Linguistics 7(3-4):152-194.

1934   Narrow Transcription of Central American. Le Maitre Phonetique 46:50.

1935   Pomo Création Myth. Journal of American Folklore 48(189):203-262.

1937a   Cantonese Dialect of Chinese. Le Maitre Phonetique. 60:69-70.

1937b   American English. Le Maitre Phonetique 60:71.

1937c   Metodologia Linguistica. Cuadernos Linguisticos 4(3-4):2-15. (Republication of 1929a)

1945   Broad Transcription and the Typewriter. Le Maitre Phonetique 84:24-25.

1950a   Indians in Overalls. The Hudson Review 3(3):237-77.

1950b   [untitled poem and sketch] . The Hudson Review 3(3): 378-379.

1950c   [untitled poem and sketch]. Imagi 13(5)(2):1.

1950d   Lorca's 'Arqueros'. Nine 3(1):53.

1951   [untitled poem and sketch]. Retort 4(4):14.

1952a Don Gregorio. Nine 3(3):242-255.

1952b Seven Indian Tales. The Hudson Review 5(2):165-198.

1953 Indian Tales. New York: A. A. Wyn.

1954 Red Indian Tales. Melbourne: William Heinemann Ltd. (Republication of 1953 with a new appendix)

1956 Une Famille de Chasseurs Indiens. Paris: Stock. (Translation of 1953 by Lola Tranec)

1961 Indians in Overalls *in* The Hudson Review Anthology, Frederic Morgan, ed., pp. 3-60. New York: Random House. (Republication of 1950a)

1968 Singing for Damaagomes among the Pit River Indians *in* Every Man His Way, Alan Dundes, ed., pp. 143-149. Englewood Cliffs, N.J.: Prentice-Hall. (Excerpt from 1950a)

1973a Coyote Shaman Songs *in* America: A Prophecy, George Quasha and Jerome Rothenberg, eds., pp. 117-118. New York: Random House. (Excerpt from 1953)

1973b Indians in Overalls. San Francisco: Turtle Island Foundation. (Republication of 1950a)

1973c Coyote Man and Old Doctor Loon. Edited and with an introduction by Bob Callahan. San Francisco: Turtle Island Foundation.

1973d Racconti Indiani. Milano: Adelphi. (Translation of 1953 by Romano Mastromattei)

1974a Coyote's Bones: Selected Poetry and Prose of Jaime de Angulo. Edited by Bob Callahan. San Francisco: Turtle Island Foundation.

1974b The Lariat. San Francisco: Turtle Island Foundation.

1974c Don Bartolomeo. San Francisco: Turtle Island Foundation. (Republication of 1925e)

1974d Achumawi Sketches. Journal of California Anthropology 1(1):80-85.

1975a   The Creation, The Water-Spirit and the Deer, Portrait of a Young Shaman, The Gilak Monster and his Sister the Ceremonial Drum, Shaman Songs. Alcheringa/Ethnopoetics n.s. 1(1):7-26.

1975b   The Achumawi Life-Force. Journal of California Anthropology 2(1):60-63. (Translation and excerpt from 1928d)

1975c   Old Time Stories. Mulch 3(3):47-59.

1976a   Old Time Stories, Volume 1: Shabegok. Edited by Bob Callahan. San Francisco: Turtle Island Foundation.

1976b   Old Time Stories, Volume 2: How the World Was Made. Edited by Bob Callahan. San Francisco: Turtle Island Foundation.

1976c   Indian Tales. London: Abacus. (Republication of 1953 with a new introduction)

1977   Old Dixie and Red Trail of the Setting Sun. New World Journal 1(2/3):36-42. (Translation and excerpt from 1928d)

1977b   Racconti Indiani. Milano: A. Mondadori. (Republication of 1973d)

1979   The Jaime de Angulo Reader. Edited by Bob Callahan. San Francisco: Turtle Island Foundation.

1983   Indianer im Overall. Munchen: Trickster Verlag. (Translation of 1950a by Mignon Scanzoni with a biographical sketch by Gui de Angulo as an appendix)

1984   Indian Tales. Munchen: Trickster Verlag. (Translation of 1953 into German by Werner Petermann).

1985   The Witch. Jaime in Taos: The Taos Papers of Jaime de Angulo; Compiled with a Biographical Introduction by Gui de Angulo. San Francisco: City Lights Books.

N.D.   Conversational texts in Achumawi. Unpublished manuscript, Boas Collection, American Philosophical Society.

N.D.   Non-technical Description of Achumawi. Unpublished manuscript, Boas Collection, American Philosophical Society.

N.D.   Reminiscences of an Achumawi Youth. Unpublished manuscript, Boas Collection, American Philosophical Society.

N.D.   Does Achumawi Belong to the Hokan Family? Unpublished manuscript, Boas Collection, American Philosophical Society.

N.D.   The Comparison Between the Semasiologies of the so-called Hokan Family (Pomo and Achumawi). Unpublished manuscript, Boas Collection, American Philosophical Society.

N.D.   Conversational Text in Atsugewi. Unpublished manuscript, Boas Collection, American Philosophical Society.

N.D.   [Mythological Text in Atsugewi]. Unpublished manuscript, Boas Collection, American Philosophical Society.

N.D.   Brevisimas notas sobre el idioma Chatino para el uso de los textos. Unpublished manuscript, Boas Collection, American Philosophical Society.

N.D.   [Chichimeco texts]. Unpublished manuscript, Boas Collection, American Philosophical Society.

N.D.   Cuento del Pescador. Unpublished manuscript, Boas Collection, American Philosophical Society.

N.D.   Cuento y frases en idioma Chontal. Unpublished manuscript, Boas Collection, American Philosophical Society.

N.D.   Brevisimas notas sobre el idioma Cuicateco. Unpublished manuscript, Boas Collection, American Philosophical Society.

N.D.   [Tfalati Kalapuya Semasiology] . Unpublished manuscript, Boas Collection, American Philosophical Society.

N.D.   Autobiography in Tfalati Kalapuya. Unpublished manuscript, Boas Collection, American Philosophical Society.

N.D.   Sample of Atfalatin-Yamhalla Dialect of Kalapuya. Unpublished manuscript, Boas Collection, American Philosophical Society.

N.D.   Konomihu Vocabulary, Obtained at Salem, Oregon. Unpublished manuscript, Boas Collection, American Philosophical Society.

N.D.   The Patwin Language. Unpublished manuscript, Boas Collection, American Philosophical Society.

N.D.   The Pomo Language. II. Yukaya Dialect. Unpublished manuscript, Boas Collection, American Philosophical Society.

N.D.   Pomo Semasiology. Unpublished manuscript, Boas Collection, American Philosophical Society.

N.D.   The Reminiscences of a Pomo Chief. Unpublished manuscript, Boas Collection, American Philosophical Society.

N.D.   Cuento Mazateco: cuento de venado y de sapes. Unpublished manuscript, Boas Collection, American Philosophical Society.

N.D.   Brevisimas notas sobre la lengua Mixe para el uso de los textos. Unpublished manuscript, Boas Collection, American Philosophical Society.

N.D.   Mixe text. Unpublished manuscript, Boas Collection, American Philosophical Society.

N.D.   Notes on the Mixe language (Oaxaca, Mexico). Unpublished manuscript, Boas Collection, American Philosophical Society.

N.D.   [Mixteco tones and Morphological Comments]. Unpublished manuscript, Boas Collection, American Philosophical Society.

N.D.   [Shasta Sample]. Unpublished manuscript, Boas Collection, American Philosophical Society.

N.D.   [Taos texts and Grammatical Notes]. Unpublished manuscript, Boas Collection, American Philosophical Society.

N.D.   Estudio Grammatical de las lenguas de la familia Zapoteca. Unpublished manuscript, Boas Collection, American Philosophical Society.

N.D.   [Zapotec texts in Miahuatec dialect]. Unpublished manuscript, Boas Collection, American Philosophical Society.

N.D.   [Zapotecan texts]. Unpublished manuscript, Boas Collection, American Philosophical Society.

N.D.   What is Language? [version 1] Unpublished manuscript, in the possession of Gui de Angulo.

N.D.   What is Language? [version 2] Unpublished manuscript, de Angulo Collection, University of California at Los Angeles.

N.D.   What is Language? [version 3] Unpublished manuscript, de Angulo Collection, University of California at Los Angeles, and Turtle Island Press Collection, University of California at Santa Cruz.

N.D.   The Achumawi. Unpublished manuscript, de Angulo Collection, University of California at Los Angeles.

N.D.   The Androgynes. Unpublished manuscript, de Angulo Collection, University of California at Los Angeles, and Turtle Island Press Collection, University of California at Santa Cruz.

N.D.   The Witch. Unpublished manuscript, de Angulo Collection, University of California at Los Angeles.

N.D.   Songs of Myself. Unpublished manuscript, de Angulo Collection, University of California at Los Angeles.

N.D.   Songs of the Hillside. Unpublished manuscript, de Angulo Collection, University of California at Los Angeles.

N.D.   Songs of the Shaman. Unpublished manuscript, de Angulo Collection, University of California at Los Angeles.

N.D.   Lorca Translations. Unpublished manuscript, de Angulo Collection, University of California at Los Angeles.

N.D.   Old Time Stories. Manuscript of the radio broadcasts, de Angulo Collection, University of California at Los Angeles.

N.D.   Fray Luis and the Devil. Two versions of the manuscript, one of which has remained unpublished, de Angulo Collection, University of California at Los Angeles.

N.D.   The Gilak steals Hawk's wife. Unpublished manuscript, de Angulo Collection, University of California at Los Angeles.

N.D.   Marijuana. Unpublished manuscript, Turtle Island Press Collection, University of California at Santa Cruz.

N.D.   Achumawi Kinship Systems. Museum of Anthropology Archives, Document 200, University of California at Berkeley.

de Angulo, Jaime and William Ralganal Benson
1932   The Creation Myth of the Pomo Indians. Anthropos 27(1-2):261-274; 27(5-6):779-795.

de Angulo, Jaime and M. Beclard d'Harcourt
1931   La Musique des Indiens de la Californie du Nord. Journal de la Societe des Americanistes de Paris n.s. 23:189-228.

de Angulo, Jaime and L. S. Freeland
1925   The Chontal Language (Dialect of Tequixistlan). Anthropos 20(5-6):1032-1052.

1928   Miwok and Pomo Myths. Journal of American Folklore 41(160):232-252.

1929a   A New Religious Movement in North-Central California. American Anthropologist 31(2):265-70.

1929b   Notes on the Northern Paiute of California. Journal de la Societe des Americanistes de Paris n.s. 21:313-335.

1931a   The Achumawi Language. International Journal of American Linguistics 6(2):77-120.

1931b   Two Achumawi Tales. Journal of American Folklore 44(172): 125-136.

1931c   Karok Texts. International Journal of American Linguistics 6(3-4):194-226.

1935   The Zapotekan Linguistic Group: A Comparative Study of Chinanteco, Choco, Mazateco, Cuicateco, Mixteco, Chatino, and especially of Zapoteco proper and its dialects. International Journal of American Linguistics 8(1):1-38; 8(2):111-130.

N.D.   Conversational text in Achumawi. Unpublished manuscript, Boas Collection, American Philosophical Society.

N.D.   Achumawi texts. Unpublished manuscript, Boas Collection, American Philosophical Society.

N.D.   Appendix of Addenda and Corrigenda to the Grammar of the Achumawi Language. Unpublished manuscript, Boas Collection, American Philosophical Society.

N.D. The Atsugewi Language. Unpublished manuscript, Boas Collection, American Philosophical Society.

N.D. The Tfalati Dialect of Kalapuya. Unpublished Manuscript, Boas Collection, American Philosophical Society.

N.D. Comparison Between Tfalati Kalapuya and Chinook Jargon. Unpublished manuscript, Boas Collection, American Philosophical Society.

N.D. The 'Clear Lake' Dialect of the Pomo Language in North-Central California. Unpublished manuscript, Boas Collection, American Philosophical Society.

N.D. The Shasta Language. Unpublished manuscript, Boas Collection, American Philosophical Society.

N.D. A Sketch of the Taos Language. Unpublished manuscript, Boas Collection, American Philosophical Society.

N.D. A Short Vocabulary in Yurok. Unpublished manuscript, Boas Collection, American Philosophical Society.

N.D. The Hangover Cookbook. Unpublished manuscript, de Angulo Collection, University of California at Los Angeles.

de Angulo, Jaime and Hans J. Uldall
1932 Pomo. Le Maitre Phonetique 37:506.

CITY LIGHTS PUBLICATIONS

Ginsberg, Allen. *PLUTONIAN ODE (Pocket Poets #40)*
Ginsberg, Allen. *REALITY SANDWICHES (Pocket Poets #18)*
Herron, Don. *THE LITERARY WORLD OF SAN FRANCISCO &
ITS ENVIRONS*
Hirschman, Jack. *LYRIPOL (Pocket Poets #34)*
Horowitz, Michael. *BIG LEAGUE POETS*
Kerouac, Jack. *BOOK OF DREAMS*
Kerouac, Jack. *SCATTERED POEMS (Pocket Poets #28)*
Kovic, Ron. *AROUND THE WORLD IN EIGHT DAYS*
La Duke, Betty. *COMPANERAS: Women, Art, & Social Change
in Latin America*
Lamantia, Philip. *BECOMING VISIBLE (Pocket Poets #39)*
Lamantia, Philip. *MEADOWLARK WEST*
Lamantia, Philip. *SELECTED POEMS (Pocket Poets #20)*
Lowry, Malcolm. *SELECTED POEMS (Pocket Poets #17)*
Lucebert. *NINE DUTCH POETS (Pocket Poets #42)*
Ludlow, Fitzhugh. *THE HASHEESH EATER*
McDonough, Kay. *ZELDA*
Moore, Daniel. *BURNT HEART*
Mrabet, Mohammed. *M'HASHISH*
Murguía, A. *VOLCAN: Poems from Central America*
Newton, Huey & Ericka Huggins. *INSIGHTS & POEMS*
O'Hara, Frank. *LUNCH POEMS (Pocket Poets #19)*
Olson, Charles. *CALL ME ISHMAEL*
Orlovsky, Peter. *CLEAN ASSHOLE POEMS & SMILING VEGETABLE
SONGS (Pocket Poets #37)*
Pickard, Tom. *GUTTERSNIPE*
Plymell, Charles. *THE LAST OF THE MOCCASINS*
Poe, Edgar Allan. *THE UNKNOWN POE*
Prévert, Jacques. *PAROLES (Pocket Poets #9)*
Rey-Rosa, Rodrigo. *THE BEGGAR'S KNIFE*
Rigaud, Milo. *SECRETS OF VOODOO*
Rips, Geoffrey. *UNAMERICAN ACTIVITIES*
Rosemont, Franklin. *SURREALISM & ITS POPULAR ACCOMPLICES*
Sanders, Ed. *INVESTIGATIVE POETRY*
Shepard, Sam. *FOOL FOR LOVE*
Shepard, Sam. *MOTEL CHRONICLES*
Snyder, Gary. *THE OLD WAYS*
Solomon, Carl. *MISHAPS PERHAPS*
Solomon, Carl. *MORE MISHAPS*
Voznesensky, Andrei. *DOGALYPSE (Pocket Poets #29)*
Waldman, Anne. *FAST SPEAKING WOMAN (Pocket Poets #33)*
Waley, Arthur. *THE NINE SONGS*
Yevtushenko, Yevgeni. *RED CATS (Pocket Poets #16)*